A WEEKEND IN THE COUNTRY
Seasonal Recipes and Ideas for Relaxed Entertaining

PHOTOGRAPHY BY LINDA BURGESS

TEXT BY SALLY ANNE SCOTT

PRENTICE HALL PRESS

New York London Toronto Sydney Tokyo Singapore

PRENTICE HALL PRESS
15 Columbus Circle
New York, New York 10023

Originally published in Great Britain by Conran Octopus Limited,
37 Shelton Street, London WC2H 9HN as
Recipes for a perfect country weekend.

Library of Congress Catalog Card Number: 91-53075

ISBN 0-13-951781-2

The publishers would like to thank Fergus Cochrane Antiques, 570 King's
Road, London SW3 2DY and the Gallery of Antique Costume and Textiles,
2 Church Street, London NW8.

Art Director   Mary Evans
Art Editor   Kit Johnson
Project Editor   Denise Bates
Recipe Editor   Lewis Esson
Americanizer   Norma MacMillan
Production   Jackie Kernaghan
Photographic Stylist   Debbie Patterson
Home Economist (photography)   Jane Suthering
Home Economist (testing)   Valerie Barrett

Manufactured in Hong Kong

10   9   8   7   6   5   4   3   2   1

First Prentice Hall Press Edition

Contents

Foreword 7

The Weekend 10

Foreword

I have to be perfectly honest and say that the original inspiration for this book was born one gloomy day in my kitchen in London. Being a city person, I often fantasized about the delights of those long, comforting country weekends, spent being totally spoilt by friends. On that particular day I imagined all the ingredients which it would take to make my weekend in the country a complete treat. Tantalizing images of cool bluebell woods filled my mind's eye; this led me on to the bed I would sleep in – a four-poster with soft, sweet-smelling linen; while from the window there would be the view of a garden spread out like a Persian rug, with a rich profusion of roses.

As I dreamed on, the aromas of the food I would like to eat during my weekend wafted into my senses, tempting me even further. I felt ready for every meal, experiencing that hunger which only exists away from home, that has been sharpened by brisk country walks, sharp fresh air and eager anticipation. I was impatient for loving meals of hearty soups, squeaky-fresh vegetables, golden roasts, comforting home-made breads and lots of fresh herbs and salads with that 'just pulled from the earth' taste. And this food was enjoyed in friendly rooms filled with flowers and glowing fires. Finally, stretched out in front of a log fire, the warmth flowed over me – all worries faded and I knew I was in the heart of the country, surrounded by friends.

Now, with the project completed, we have created this dream. The photography of the book was a great joy, the friends warm and the food delightful. I hope we have extended to everyone an invitation to a country weekend.

LINDA BURGESS

The Weekend

Country weekends initially became a necessary part of my life to counteract the stresses and strains of a hectic city existence. Fifteen years ago we bought a beautiful but derelict Georgian farmhouse in Somerset, England. Gradually, as the house was renovated, friends began to take advantage of the very relaxing and unpressurized atmosphere and the house acquired a name that has stuck when, twelve years ago, we were visited by two designer friends, who staggered in bearing a lovely lamp for the porch with the inscription "Hornblotton Hilton." The weekends that followed over the years, during which this became our permanent home, evolved quite simply through getting to know the locals, sampling their produce and learning the history of our sleepy Somerset hamlet and its environs.

Country walking is now a part of my life from which I gain enormous pleasure. Nature's glorious free booty, which should never be taken for granted, allows me to pick posies of wild flowers to put beside a guest bed, pluck hedgerow fruits to make into interesting preserves for tea, or gather mushrooms on a misty morning to serve minutes later for a hearty breakfast.

As a working lady and subsequently a working mum, I have always put organization and the preparation of the food in advance high on my list of priorities. Careful balancing of meals, too, has always been a firm objective. I interweave masses of fresh herbs in a meal high in cholesterol, for example, or use sea vegetables and organically grown produce for necessary minerals. Variety in cooking styles also aids the busy cook. Steaming, stir-frying, baking and even barbecueing all produce a wide selection of different tastes and textures. The love and patience that go into food preparation are reflected in its taste and presentation. Conversely, grumpy hostesses prepare grumpy food!

Imagine my delight on being asked to use my beloved home and my lifestyle for this book. I found that the text and the recipes flowed easily and on meeting Linda Burgess I felt that her affinity with the country, her mental attitude and her stunning photography meant for me a joyous meeting of souls. The experience of writing this book has been one of my most pleasurable to date.

BOOTS SCOTT

CAMELLIAS (*previous page*)

It was Bacon who said that "Proverbs are the philosophy of the common man" (John Gerard's *Herbal*, 1597). Proverbs grow from the continuity of things, indicating a trend or a cause and effect, and to most country folk cloud formation, wind direction, animal and insect behavior, the elements, the seasons and all that they hold are forces which help direct their daily lives. There can often be a heavy penalty to pay when Mother Nature's potent signs are ignored – crop failure, drought, and disease all conspire against those who mistrust the signals that she puts out for us to see. Rooks nesting high herald a good dry summer, free from high winds. Swallows returning early from their warm winter refuges invariably means temperate weather will follow. "Oak before ash, in for a splash – ash before oak, in for a soak." "Holly berries before the end of September – a winter to remember." Almost without exception these observations which have become country lore still hold good. There is much to see, much to learn in the country, the place where real life stands naked and raw for everyone to benefit from, provided they see with their eyes and hear with their ears and smell with their noses. This is not quite as simple as it sounds, when one realizes the abundance of seeing, hearing, smelling, and learning to be done. Any time spent in the country plays a valuable part in that learning process, and a weekend, although short, can be utilized to great effect. The dawn chorus, farmyards, rivers and streams, meadows and woods all hold wonderful opportunities to excite the mind and enchant children in particular with everlasting memories. The sheer beauty of a landscape or the peace and tranquility of a spot untarnished by the two-legged species can be enough to soothe many visitors.

INVITATION TO A WALK
A well-trodden pathway holds out an irresistible invitation to long country rambles.

WELCOMING TOUCHES & GIFTS

Small things from the heart of the host give enormous pleasure. Preparing small gifts can for the most part be incorporated into the daily domestic routine. And they are often free, with many ingredients coming from the hedgerows, gardens, and woods. It is my experience that simplicity wins hands down in any competition. The small posy of wild or domestic flowers, rather than an elaborate floral display, or a little basket of seasonal fruit in the bedroom, along with a glass, slices of fresh lemon and lime, and a bottle of mineral water, make a comforting impression on arrival. Most people enjoy being spoiled and this can easily be done without too much effort. When washing the sheets, for example, put lavender water or rose water into the rinse, rather than a conventional household product. Herb pillows take no time to make and are conducive to relaxing sleep. In high summer, when the herbs are in full flower and the weather is hot and dry, encourage your guests to pick their own herbs and make these little pillows.

Herb Pillows

Pretty material (preferably linen or cotton),
measuring about 10 x 5 inches
about 2 heaped tbsp dried herbs (lavender,
thyme, rosemary, or a mixture)
rubber band
ribbon
essential oils

Fold the material across in half to make a square and sew up the sides, leaving the top open. Fill the pillow with dried herbs of your choice. Secure the top tightly with a rubber band, then cover this with a pretty ribbon tied in a bow. To give the pillows even more aroma, add a few drops of essential oils with the herbs.

Children in particular love little projects that remind them of the places that they have visited. Making pot pourri with fresh petals and herbs is also a delightful activity.

Pot Pourri

Always pick fresh petals or herbs for pot pourri mid-morning on a dry, sunny day, when the flowers are completely open.

fresh petals or herbs
cheesecloth or thin linen
ground orris root
good-quality talcum powder or essential oils

Remove any green stem and the white part of the petal (the heel). Spread the flowers or herbs out on the piece of cheesecloth (or thin linen), making sure that the petals or sprigs do not touch one another, and place out of direct sunlight in an airy, but not drafty room. If possible, suspend the cloth between the backs of 2 chairs, say, to allow a good circulation of air.

Several days later, when the petals or sprigs are crisp to the touch, store in sealed glass jars until ready for use. When making up a bowl of pot pourri, sprinkle in some ground orris root, strong good-quality talcum powder, or drops of essential oils (more expensive) for a longer-lasting perfume. Turn the petals constantly for maximum effect and replenish as required. (It is a good idea to cover bowls of pot pourri at night or when away for long periods to preserve their aroma and keep them free of dust.)

ROSE POT POURRI
Fresh blooms enhance a bowl of pot pourri.

Recreate the memory of a country show or fair for guests by making special little jars of jam, jelly, or preserve when you are making a large batch anyway. A piece of ribbon tied around the jar or a pretty cloth top will always produce a smile. Throughout the seasons, there is an abundance of choice for small gifts. Petal and herb vinegars, herb oils, dried flower posies, homemade chocolates, cordials from the hedgerows, and nut wreaths for Christmas decorations are just a few of the possibilities. If they are creatively designed and packaged, these simple, inexpensive items can be transformed into little treasures.

Petal Vinegars

petals such as rose, violet, nasturtium, or elderflower
white wine vinegar or cider vinegar

Remove the white heel and any green stem from the petals (use scissors to avoid unnecessary bruising – small manicure scissors are particularly effective), place the petals in a sterilized bottle or jar, and pour in the vinegar. Use white wine vinegar for pastel-colored petals and cider vinegar for more vibrant colors. Leave to steep for 4 weeks, preferably on a sunny windowsill.

Using foliage as a garnish for food is something that can be done all year round. Flowers and petals, leaves, and even feathers all help to create a visually pleasing effect. Try grape leaves under your cheeses, or horse-chestnut leaves with the chestnuts still attached to create an autumnal feel to accompany dishes that warm cold hands and toes. Silverweed, an enchanting edible wild leaf with a dark green color and silver tint, makes a welcome change from parsley. Flower heads floating in a glass bowl or in shallow glass dishes make for interesting discussions, and are easily changed when the flowers start to wilt.

Herb Vinegars

2 cups vinegar (mild for mild-flavored herbs, strong for the more pungent)
2 oz crushed garlic (about 7-8 cloves)
about 2 tbsp flowering herbs, lightly bruised

Bring the vinegar to just below boiling point. Put the garlic with the herbs in a heatproof sealable container. Pour the vinegar over the garlic and herbs, leave to cool a little, and then seal the container while still warm. Leave for 3 weeks, shaking or turning twice weekly. At the end of this time, strain to remove the old herbs and add a few sprigs of fresh. Keep in a cool, dry place.

It is possible to be really creative with these floral displays and arrangements and to use just about anything that is on hand. Decorations using bits of bark, empty snail shells, and dried wild mushrooms (if you can resist the temptation to eat them) are further possibilities. Pumpkins and other small squashes and gourds make a glorious table decoration, interspersed with autumn vines, Japonica quince, medlars, and rosy red apples. Add green walnuts and hazelnuts or filberts in their husks and you have a wonderfully colorful, original display. Lichen and moss are all fun to collect on a country ramble, and even more fun when used to create a decoration as a semi-permanent reminder of that walk.

HERB VINEGARS *(above right)*
Vinegars flavored with fresh herbs have a multitude of uses. As well as in vinaigrettes, you can use them to flavor sauces or add a splash or two when cooking fish.

WEEKEND ACTIVITIES

If possible, have suitable literature, such as guide books, available in the house, showing times of opening of local places of interest. The local paper is a good source of information, and sporting events, festivals, fairs, bazaars, and farmers' markets are usually great favorites. Characters abound, and there is invariably something to please everyone. Some town folk feel a sense of unease when confronted with the odd silence of the countryside, so the chance to get back into the bustle and noise of what they have left behind – although nicely diluted – makes them feel more at home. Often people will head straight for the homemade produce stalls at these events, endorsing the belief that produce from the home and the countryside still rates high above that available from the supermarket. For those guests who prefer peace and solitude, a walk along a beach or in the woods can be added to the agenda.

Binoculars that children may use give enormous pleasure and of course a telescope to roam the wondrously bright starry skies would put most people in heaven. Bird-watching and astronomy hobbies may start from these early times spent learning. In addition, shell- and rock-collecting might prove to be of lasting interest.

Recommend to your guests on acceptance of your invitation that they bring clothing to fit the season, and, indeed, to be prepared for inclement weather. It is a rare host who is able to furnish every single guest with full weatherproof gear to fit every size. Lack of this important equipment can mean not being able to go somewhere or do something in the rain. Walking or visiting places during a country rain is not the same as doing it in town, and the

refreshing feel of rain on one's skin and hair can have a therapeutic effect. Children, particularly, love to be able to splash through muddy puddles in fields and get soaked from the black cloud hovering so close they can almost touch it, only to come back to the warmth of an open log fire and feel the tingles as they dry out. Encourage them to enjoy these sensations – they may not have the opportunity to experience them very often.

The natural world has many more delights for children. Let them put dead bugs into matchboxes to take back to show their friends. When woodlice, butterflies, dragonflies, spiders, and bees come to the end of their natural life, it is both educational and interesting for a child to be able to look at them close up.

A genuinely exciting little project, easily organized for both children and grown-ups – though not necessarily both at the same time – is to go star-gazing. On a crisp autumn or winter evening when the air is clear and the stars look near, put a blanket on the ground to sit on and then wrap up warmly in more blankets or even sleeping bags. The magic of lying flat on your back, looking up into eternity, wishing on stars, and spotting well-known constellations is a memory from my own childhood that I cherish to this day.

Spotting glowworms is another activity that brings delight to the faces of young and old. Again, warm clothing, a clear night, and a good flashlight are standard equipment for this adventure. Try to resist the temptation to put the glowworms in a jar – they are rare little creatures and should be left to multiply. Either pre-meal or post-meal exercises like these create a topic of conversation for the evening, and a subject for the children to discuss for years to come.

A SIMPLE WELCOME
Little touches like fresh fruit and flowers or foliage in the bedroom are often all that is needed to make guests feel special.

FEELING AT HOME

No matter how well the guests are known, most people feel a sense of unease if their host or hostess is constantly bustling about. Planning of the weekend menu and activities, as well as any baking done beforehand will ensure that panic is kept to a minimum. You still need a flexible schedule to suit all in the party, however. Guests should not be made to feel that they have to adhere rigidly to your minutely planned timetable.

Often people like to feel that they are contributing. Let them set the table, load the dishwasher, or wash the dishes if they offer. For those hosts who like to do it all themselves, always make sure that your guests are alternatively occupied. Encouraging them to wander around the garden with a drink before dinner leaves time for you to make the table look lovely; or suggest that they could pick some flowers or light and trim some candles. Deploy those who invade your kitchen, the place guests usually enjoy most. Their taste buds are tickled by the smells pervading the house, and it can be extremely irritating to have to dance around those static bodies draped over the countertops or, worst of all (and most popular), blocking the main doorways. Suggesting that your guests vacate the kitchen is often difficult – social chat and a pleasant sense of well-being conspire against easy removal. Organizing little projects or jobs before meals is a useful way to get space to yourself at an important time!

Many old houses in the country have their own, sometimes irritating, idiosyncrasies – those creaking floorboards under the bed, the cistern that sounds like flood gates opening every time it's flushed, the second-to-bottom stair that squeaks in the night as you try to creep past it. It's fun to have nicely written lists in the bedrooms detailing all the minor horrors that might be encountered if your guests get the munchies in the middle of the night, for instance, or simply cannot get to sleep and want to go for a wander. It's highly embarrassing to be heard creeping down the stairs, or to wake the whole household by flushing a very noisy toilet after an early morning visit, and full knowledge of the traps and pitfalls can take the edge off a potentially worrying incident for your guests. After all, a successful weekend in the country is about enjoyment and relaxation, for both hosts and guests, so it's worth spending some time and thought on creating the most conducive atmosphere possible.

Spring

The vernal equinox marks the beginning of spring, a time of blossom and birdsong, cowslips and crocuses, dandelions and daffodils. The memory of gray winter months fades quickly as the anticipation of summer is smelled in the nippy spring air and seen in the lively activity of small animals and birds, as they prepare for the first nest-building and mating of the season. On the ground and in the hedgerow there are frenetic gatherings of all kinds of materials. Moss and straw, sticks and mud, dead leaves and feathers are all utilized in incredible feats of construction, be it the ragged crow's nest, the beautiful soft feather bed of the tit, or the mud dome of the swallow. All are created with unending energy and fussed with until perfection is attained.

NEW BEGINNINGS (*above*)

FLORAL TAPESTRY (*previous page*)

Hibernating animals stir from their warm winter beds, beckoned by the warmth of spring sunshine gently invading the den that has kept them safe throughout the cold preceding months. Instinct and hunger ease them into action, and fields and forests slowly become alive again with sleepy bodies going in search of food.

Snowdrops and violets, primroses and grape hyacinths weave gentle patterns on banks and in woods, their colors such a pleasing sight. Pale green shoots and virgin leaves pop out from their protective covers, changing the landscape so very gently.

April sees the return of the swallows, a most cheery sight as they soar and dive, performing quite incredible aerial feats, and frog, newt, and toad tadpoles are hatching in the still waters of ponds and pools. Encourage friends to notice these natural clues of the countryside. Spring-time vegetation is young enough not to obscure records of where animals have been, but remember also, when you are out walking one of the most important rules of the country code – that of shutting all gates behind you. Never drop any litter, which could easily choke animals, and never pick any endangered species of wild flora.

If you get the age-old spring-cleaning desire, clean your hard-working chimney by throwing about ½ pound of saltpeter onto the hot flames once a week for six weeks. It will loosen all the soot, which then burns away, saving you a call from the chimney sweep. Another spring-cleaning tip is to dip an ordinary feather in turpentine and wipe it around the corners of your rooms to persuade insects, and in particular spiders, to lay their eggs elsewhere.

Suggest to children that they make egg-shell collages, or stick spring flowers onto boiled eggs that can then be varnished. Make natural dyes by boiling vegetable and plant material in water until it is the color you want. Then strain the liquid and soak the eggs in it. Use onion skins, heather, quack grass flowers, and straw for yellow, pine cones and elder bark for browny-black, and birch bark for purple.

Dandelions can be gathered to make wine, but leave the elegant, and sadly still rare, cowslip where you find her. Sticky buds find a place in floral displays, and bright green moss and silver-gray lichen are wonderful in table decorations. Enjoy the sunshine yellow of the flowering quack grass, side by side with buds of broom and the blossom of the crab apple. Use blackthorn blossom to dress your mantelpiece, but be careful when picking it and always use garden shears, for the thorns are large and vicious. If you do get stabbed, make a paste from a little water mixed with baking soda. The paste should be thick enough to coat your finger and you can then cover it with a loose bandage. This will draw out the thorn and make its removal much easier. Soak the finger in warm water before extracting the thorn with sterilized tweezers.

Petal ice cubes look delightful in drinks and petal or herb vinegars (see page 14) make wonderful dressings, as well as attractive presents.

Petal Ice Cubes

This novel idea is a simple way of making drinks look very special.

Simply add one petal per ice cube to the tray before freezing. Rose petals are particularly good for this purpose. Other useful spring flowers are borage, with its sky-blue petals, comfrey, small pansies, cherry, apple, and pear blossoms, primroses, and violets.

Collect carragheen from the seashore, rinsing it thoroughly to remove tiny particles of shell, then dry it to use in the coming months for a real taste of the sea. Such sea vegetables, I feel sure, will become an important food source as we get used to their unfamiliar but exciting taste. Purple-red dulse is another sea vegetable, which can also be bought. If you collect it fresh from the seashore, roast it in a moderate oven until it is bone dry and crumbly, then either place it in a bag and crush with a rolling pin, or use a pestle and mortar to reduce it to a fine powder. Store it in a glass – not plastic – screw-top jar and use it as a condiment for soups and salads. Samphire, too, is a delicious sea vegetable which good fish merchants often stock when it is in season (see page 63). Try tender young mallow leaves quickly deep-fried as another unusual vegetable.

If you are lucky enough to have discovered where morel mushrooms grow, collect and dry them to enjoy later, perhaps out of season as a real treat. These truly wonderfully flavored fungi may be used to great effect both fresh and dried. Growing mainly on sandy soil (mostly above chalk), once you discover a good spot for them guard it with your life. The short growing period (March-April) means that they are usually in short supply. If intending to dry them, do give them a chance to develop to a good size before picking them as they shrink considerably in the process.

Drying Morels

fresh morels
paper towel
large-eyed darning needle
coarse thread

Morels are renowned for providing homes for mini-beasts, so shake them well first, then slice them in half vertically and wash them very carefully. Place the halves on a piece of paper towel and pat them gently until they are dry.

Using a large-eyed darning needle and some coarse thread, string them one behind the other on the thread a few inches apart, piercing them through their fleshiest part, and then hang them in a warm, dry place in the kitchen or in the airing cupboard. After about 3 days they should be crisp. Remove them from the thread and place them in dry, sterilized glass containers and seal. When needed for cooking, simply soak them in water for 40 minutes before use (use the soaking water in stocks and soups).

EARLY MORNING LIGHT
Sunlight highlights the delicacy of parrot tulips.

MENUS *for Spring*

BREAKFAST
Muesli Bread (p. 24)
Chunky Seville Marmalade (p. 24)
Poached Haddock on Muffins
(p. 36 and p. 26)
Deviled Kidneys (p. 41)

LIGHT LUNCH
Jerusalem Artichoke Soup (p. 32)
Paupiettes of Beef (p. 40)
Noodles with Primrose Leaves (p. 33)

LUNCH
Tenerife Potatoes with Herb Sauce (p. 33)
Seafood Soup (p. 36)
Tangerine Ice Cream (p. 31)

TEA
Griddle Cakes (p. 24)
Quick Orange and Lemon Cake (p. 29)
Chocolate Cake with Fudge Layers (p. 26)

LIGHT SUPPER
Poached Eggs on Sorrel Nests (p. 28)
or
Flower Galettes (p. 28)
Seared Lamb Slices (p. 40)
Leeks Vinaigrette (p. 34)
Crunchy Cabbage with Cumin (p. 32)

DINNER
Scallops with Lime Sauce (p. 39)
Chicken with Coconut and Lemon
(p. 43)
Almond Broccoli (p. 32)
Hedgehog Potatoes (p. 33)
Rhubarb and Maple Syrup Sorbet
(p. 29)
Langues-de-chat (p. 29)

PREPARATION

Muesli Bread

WITH NUTS AND APPLE

Makes one large loaf
Preparation: 30 mins, 1 hr ahead
Cooking: 45-55 mins, plus cooling

3 cups 100% stoneground
wholewheat flour
1 tsp salt
1 cup rolled oats
1 tbsp golden raisins (unsulfured, if
possible)
½ tbsp finely chopped nuts
1 tbsp freshly grated apple
2 tbsp butter
½ oz compressed yeast or 1 package active
dry yeast
1 heaping tbsp honey

In a large bowl, mix the flour and the salt with the oats, raisins, nuts, and apple. Rub in the butter, blending it well.

Into a small bowl, put the yeast and mix it well with the slightly warmed honey, then add ⅔ cup lukewarm water. Stir gently and leave in a warm part of the kitchen until frothy.

Add this yeast mixture to the flour mixture along with another ⅔ cup lukewarm water. Blend until the dough is soft but not sticky.

Place the dough on a cold, floured surface, cover with a dampened linen or cotton cloth, and leave the dough to rest for about 8 minutes.

Knead the dough gently and then press it into a greased 9 x 5 x 3-inch loaf pan. Mark the top with two crosses, indenting to about ½ inch. Cover with buttered wax paper and leave to rise until it reaches the rim of the pan. Preheat the oven to 400° F.

Bake for about 45-55 minutes. Remove from the oven, unmold the loaf, and leave to cool on a wire rack.

Griddle Cakes

Griddle cakes or pancakes, called drop scones or Scotch pancakes in Britain, are delicious served in the traditional way with butter and maple or other sweet syrup. But you might also like to try them spread with jam or other preserves or honey.

Makes 15-18
Preparation: 15 mins
Cooking: 4-6 mins per batch

¾ cup self-rising flour
pinch of salt
1 tbsp sugar
1 egg, lightly beaten
⅔ cup milk

Put a griddle or large heavy-based skillet over a moderate heat and leave to heat up. Meanwhile, sift the flour and the salt into a bowl and stir in the sugar. Make a well in the center and drop the egg into the well.

Gradually add the milk, working in the flour from the edges with a spoon until a smooth batter is formed. Turn this batter into a large pitcher.

Turn the heat up under the griddle or skillet and grease it with a little butter or margarine. Pour the batter into the pan in small rounds. Cook as many as can comfortably fit on the griddle or skillet.

As soon as the cakes bubble and puff on the surface and are golden on the underside (after about 2 or 3 minutes), flip them over with a spatula to brown them on the other side.

Cook the remaining cakes in the same way in subsequent batches as necessary, keeping the cooked cakes warm between the folds of a clean cloth. Serve as soon as all are cooked, with butter, jam, etc.

Chunky Seville Marmalade

I always chop the oranges quite coarsely so that the marmalade has delicious chunks of fruit in it.

Makes 10 lb
Preparation: 50 mins
Cooking: about 3 hrs, plus cooling

3 lb Seville oranges
juice of 2 lemons
6 lb (13½ cups) sugar

Use unsprayed oranges or remove any wax from them by scrubbing in warm soapy water. Rinse them well and then dry thoroughly.

Using a vegetable peeler or a paring knife, pare off the outer peel downward in thin strips, leaving behind any bitter white membrane. Scissor these strips of peel into ¼-inch pieces. Cut the oranges in half and squeeze out the juice,

reserving the seeds. Cut away all the white membrane and put this with the seeds into a cheesecloth bag (an old cotton pillowcase, cut down, will do). Tie up securely.

Cut the orange flesh into coarse chunks and put them into a kettle with the chopped peel and the bag of orange seeds. Add the strained orange and lemon juices. Bring the mixture to a boil over a low heat and simmer, uncovered, for about 2 hours, or until the peel is soft and the kettle contents are reduced by about half.

Remove the cheesecloth bag and add the sugar, stirring constantly until it is all dissolved. Turn up the heat and boil the mixture rapidly for about 45 minutes, until gel point is reached. (Use an all-purpose thermometer to gauge gel point at 220°F. Alternatively, drop a teaspoon of the mixture onto a cold saucer: the skin will wrinkle when prodded with your finger once gel point has been reached.) Skim immediately, then leave to cool and settle for about 30 minutes.

Stir the marmalade, if necessary, to distribute the peel evenly, then pour the

Chunky Seville Marmalade

marmalade into warm, dry, sterilized jars and cover with disks of waxed paper. When cool, seal with metal tops or plastic wrap secured with rubber bands or string.

Label (including the date) and store in a cool, dry place. Note: For long storage, it is advisable to process jars of hot marmalade in a boiling-water bath.

Muffins

Makes 18
Preparation: 15 mins
Cooking: 20 mins

1¼ cups milk
1 tbsp pure honey
1 tbsp molasses
1 tsp baking soda
¾ cup unbleached all-purpose flour
1 cup wholewheat flour
2 cups barley flour
1 tsp baking powder
½ cup golden raisins (optional)
½ tsp salt
¾ cup raw brown sugar
2 tbsp butter

Preheat the oven to 400°F and grease 18 muffin pans with a little butter.

Place the milk in a pan, add the honey and molasses, and stir over a gentle heat to dissolve. Then add the baking soda and mix well.

Place the flours, baking powder, raisins (if using), salt, and sugar in a large bowl. Rub in the butter.

Gradually stir the warmed milk mixture into the dry mixture, beating well to incorporate smoothly.

Spoon the batter into the prepared muffin pans and bake for 20 minutes, or until risen and firm.

Remove the cooked muffins from the pans and place on a wire rack. Keep warm those to be used immediately under a clean cloth. Once cool, keep the other muffins in an airtight container or freeze them.

Chocolate Cake

WITH FUDGE LAYERS

The generous fudge filling and frosting of this cake definitely put it in the special treats category. If you would like more cake in relation to the fudge, make the same quantity of filling but double the cake quantities to make two 8-inch layers. They can then be put together as usual with fudge spread in the middle and on top of the cake.

Serves 8-10
Preparation: 15 mins
Cooking: about 30 mins, plus cooling and decorating

1 stick butter, softened
½ cup sugar
2 eggs, lightly beaten
2 tbsp unsweetened cocoa
¾ cup self-rising flour

for the fudge:
2¼ cups sugar
2 tbsp light corn syrup
4 tbsp unsalted butter
⅔ cup unsweetened cocoa

Preheat the oven to 350° F.

Line an 8-inch round cake pan with waxed paper lightly greased with butter, one piece on the bottom and a rectangle to line the sides.

Combine the butter and the sugar in a bowl and beat until light and fluffy. Incorporate the eggs a little at a time.

Blend the cocoa with enough hot water to make a smooth paste. Allow it to cool, then add this to the mixture a little at a time, alternating with spoonfuls of the flour, and beat gently to make the batter smooth after each addition.

Pour the batter into the prepared pan and smooth the top with a spatula. Bake on the middle shelf of the oven for about 25-30 minutes, or until the chocolate cake is well risen.

Meanwhile, make the fudge: put all the ingredients with 1¼ cups water in a heavy-bottomed saucepan and cook gently. Do not allow the mixture to boil until the sugar has *completely* dissolved.

Bring the mixture to a boil and place a candy thermometer in the mixture. Continue to boil it gently until the thermometer registers 238° F.

To ensure that the mixture does not stick, draw the thermometer across the top of the fudge and a wooden spoon across the bottom, but do not stir! Remove the fudge from the heat and leave to cool in the pan. Once cool, beat the fudge fiercely with the wooden spoon until smooth.

Unmold the cake onto a wire rack and remove the paper. Leave to cool.

When completely cooled, cut the cake horizontally into two equal layers and spread the bottom layer with fudge. Place the top of the cake on the layer of fudge, then coat the top of the cake with fudge. Decorate as desired.

THE OUTDOOR LIFE
As sunnier days return and new warmth invigorates the earth, the impulse to move as many activities as possible outdoors is strong. An old table set up in the garden provides the perfect base for baking.

EGGS AND CREAM

Poached Eggs on Sorrel Nests

WITH TARRAGON SAUCE

It is a delight to see the bright green spears of sorrel shooting up in the spring garden. The lemon-like sharpness of sorrel offsets beautifully the richness of the cream in this dish, for a really refreshing taste of spring.

Serves 6
Preparation: about 15 mins
Cooking: 10 mins

1½ lb sorrel leaves
6 tbsp butter
1½ cups heavy cream
2 tbsp finely chopped tarragon leaves
½ heaping tsp Dijon mustard
¾ tsp white wine vinegar
4 tomatoes, skinned and seeded
6 extra large very fresh eggs
½ tsp malt vinegar
salt and pepper
6 sprigs of tarragon, for garnish

Pick over the sorrel and remove stems as far as the middle of the leaves. Wash the leaves and pat them dry.

Place the leaves one on top of another, then roll them all into a cigar shape and cut this across into ½-inch wide strips.

Melt 4 tbsp butter in a heavy-based skillet over a moderate heat. Quickly stir the shredded sorrel into the butter and stir constantly until it reduces to a soft, creamy consistency.

Add the cream and bring quickly to a boil. Remove from the heat, adjust the seasoning, and keep warm.

Melt the remaining butter in the rinsed-out skillet over a moderate heat and add the chopped tarragon. Stir in the mustard and the white wine vinegar followed by the tomatoes and cook until soft. Press the mixture through a sieve and keep warm.

Poach the eggs in a pan of water, to which has been added the malt vinegar, until just cooked and still soft inside.

Place the sorrel in nest shapes on 6 warm plates, then put one poached egg in the middle of each nest and cover with the sauce. Garnish each with a tarragon sprig and serve.

Flower Galettes

These thin crêpes look delightful with their sprinkling of colorful flowers. It is up to you which flower heads or petals you use, but please do not pick rare wild flowers, however lovely they may look.

Nectar is a kind of fruit juice, sold in good health food shops, and is delicious poured over the galettes. Alternatively, serve with fruit preserve.

Makes about 15-20
Preparation: 15 mins, 3 hrs ahead
Cooking: 3 mins per galette

⅞ cup coconut milk
⅞ cup skim milk
3 tbsp assorted flower heads or petals (pansy, calendula, violet, primrose, dandelion, geranium)
1¼ cups unbleached all-purpose flour (or equal parts all-purpose and wholewheat)
1 tsp baking powder
¼ tsp sugar
¼ tsp salt
2 eggs, beaten
corn oil, for frying
apricot or peach nectar, to serve (optional)

Put the milks in a saucepan and add the flowers. Bring to a boil over a low heat and let simmer gently for 7 minutes. Drain the liquid into a pitcher and reserve the flowers.

Place the flour, baking powder, sugar, and salt in a blender or food processor and, using a slow pulse, gradually add the eggs and then the milk and finally the flowers. Pour the batter into a bowl, cover, and let stand in the refrigerator for about 3 hours.

Preheat a heavy crêpe pan or a small heavy-bottomed skillet, add a few drops of oil, and tilt to coat thoroughly. Cover the bottom of the pan with the batter, tilting to coat evenly, and allow to cook thoroughly until golden. Flip over and cook the other side in the same way. Transfer to a warmed serving plate, cover, and keep warm in a low oven while cooking the remaining galettes in the same way.

Serve as soon as all the galettes are ready, accompanied by apricot or peach nectar, if wished, or with any good-quality fruit preserve.

Quick Orange and Lemon Cake

Quick to make and delicious to eat. Forget the taboo of eating cake before it cools and enjoy this while it's still warm.

Serves 6-8
Preparation: 5 mins
Cooking: 40-50 mins

1 lemon
1 orange
1¼ cups self-rising flour
1 tsp baking powder
1 cup + 2 tbsp sugar
1 stick butter, softened
2 eggs
3 tbsp milk

Preheat the oven to 350°F and line a 7-inch round cake pan with waxed paper, lightly greased with butter.

Either buy unsprayed or unwaxed fruit or scrub them in warm soapy water, rinse well, and pat dry. Grate the peel of the lemon and orange, then cut each in half and squeeze the juice from one half of each. Combine the juices in a bowl.

Place all the ingredients, except the orange and lemon juice and ¼ cup of the sugar, in a blender or food processor and mix thoroughly. Pour the batter into the prepared pan and then bake for about 40-50 minutes.

Remove from the oven and leave in the pan. While still hot, sprinkle the top all over with the reserved sugar. Then drizzle over the mixture of lemon and orange juices.

Allow the cake to cool a little before serving. It's also good cold, of course.

Rhubarb and Maple Syrup Sorbet

Any syrup can be used here, but once you taste the blending of rhubarb and maple, others will not compare.

Serves 6-8
Preparation: 25 mins
Cooking: 25 mins
Freezing: about 5 hrs

9 tbsp sugar
1 lb rhubarb
2 tsp lemon juice
1 tbsp maple syrup
1 elderflower head (if available)
1 egg white

In a heavy-bottomed saucepan, dissolve the sugar in 2 tablespoons of water. Once all the sugar has dissolved, bring the mixture to a boil, then reduce the heat and simmer uncovered for about 6 minutes or until the syrup is thick. Allow to cool to room temperature, then cover and chill in the refrigerator.

Wash and trim the rhubarb and cut it into 1-inch thick slices. Put these in a pan with the lemon juice and maple syrup (and elderflower head, if available, in a cheesecloth bag), add 2 tablespoons of water, and simmer gently until the rhubarb is soft. Allow to cool.

Add the cooled sugar syrup to the rhubarb and combine in a blender until smooth. Pour this mixture into a shallow dish, cover, and freeze.

When the mixture is frozen, return to the blender, adding the egg white which has been beaten to stiff peaks, and process again until smooth. Return to the shallow dish, cover, and freeze the sorbet once more.

Serve with langues-de-chat.

Langues-de-chat

These biscuits are delicious served with all kinds of ice creams and sorbets.

Makes 24
Preparation: 10 mins
Cooking: about 6-9 mins

5 tbsp butter
½ cup sugar
whites of 2 extra large eggs, lightly beaten
⅓ cup all-purpose flour, sifted

Preheat the oven to 400°F and lightly grease a baking sheet with a little butter.

Combine the butter and sugar in a blender and process until light and fluffy. Add the egg whites and process until well combined, then stir in the flour using a metal fork.

Put this mixture in a decorating bag fitted with a small plain tube. Pipe about six 3-inch long strips on the prepared baking sheet, far enough apart to allow for the mixture spreading.

Bake for about 5-8 minutes until golden brown around the edges. Remove from the oven and allow to cool for about 1 minute before lifting off with a narrow spatula and transferring to a wire rack to cool completely.

The cookies will keep in an airtight container for several weeks. They are unsuitable for freezing.

Tangerine Ice Cream LEFT *(p. 31), Rhubarb and Maple Syrup Sorbet with Langues-de-chat* RIGHT *(overleaf)*

Tangerine Ice Cream

Satsumas or clementines can be substituted for the tangerines in this recipe.

Serves 8
Preparation: 20 mins
Cooking: 10 mins
Freezing: about 6 hrs

about 10 unwaxed tangerines
1 tsp unflavored gelatin
1¼ cups milk
1¼ cups heavy cream
1 cup + 2 tbsp sugar
2 tbsp lemon juice
¾ tsp salt

With a zester, pare off enough peel (without white membrane) from the tangerines to make 2 teaspoons of peel. Blanch the peel in boiling water for 1 minute. Allow to cool and pat dry. Peel the tangerines completely, removing all white membrane. Discard the seeds. In a food processor mash the flesh of the tangerines lightly to make about 2½ cups of pulp.

In a heatproof bowl set over boiling water or in a double boiler, dissolve the gelatin in 3 tablespoons of water. Stir the gelatin into the milk and cream, then gently stir in the remaining ingredients including the tangerine peel and pulp.

Pour into a shallow freezer container, cover, and freeze for 3 hours, until just softly frozen. Spoon this mixture into an ice-cold bowl and beat hard with a wooden spoon until it is smooth, but still frozen. Return to the freezer, cover, and freeze until firm.

Take the ice cream out of the freezer and allow it to stand at room temperature for about 10 minutes before serving.

VEGETABLES AND HERBS

Jerusalem Artichoke Soup

This thick soup could be a meal in itself served with lots of crusty bread. For a thinner consistency, use more wine or stir in some cream toward the end.

Serves 8
Preparation: 15 mins
Cooking: 30-40 mins, plus cooling

1½ lb Jerusalem artichokes
2 pints vegetable stock
4 tbsp butter
2 large onions, peeled and sliced
1½ tbsp flour
½ tsp grated nutmeg
¼ tsp ground cinnamon
salt and pepper
1¼ cups dry white wine
juice of 2 limes
chopped parsley, for garnish

Scrub the artichokes thoroughly, then put them in a large pan with the vegetable stock and bring to a boil. Reduce the heat and simmer gently until the artichokes are tender.

Melt the butter in a heavy-bottomed pan over a moderate heat and sauté the onions in it until they are translucent. Add the flour and cook thoroughly, stirring constantly.

Add the nutmeg and cinnamon, then gradually add the stock and the artichokes, stirring all the time until the mixture is well blended and smooth. Remove from the heat and allow to cool.

When cool, adjust the seasoning and purée in a blender, pulsing on and off, until smooth. Return the mixture to a low heat, add the white wine, and bring *almost* to a boil.

Serve in warmed bowls, sprinkled with the lime juice, lightly stirred, and garnished with chopped parsley.

Crunchy Cabbage

WITH CUMIN

Serves 6
Preparation: 5 mins
Cooking: about 5 mins

1½ lb white cabbage
4 tbsp butter
1 tsp ground cumin
sea salt and freshly ground black pepper

Finely shred the cabbage, place it in a colander, and rinse it well. Shake off the surplus water.

Melt the butter in a deep saucepan over a low heat. Add the cumin and cook gently for about 40 seconds.

Add the cabbage, cover the pan, and leave for about 2 minutes to settle. Stir, cover again, and shake the pan. Reduce the heat and allow the cabbage to continue cooking for a few minutes more in the butter and steam. When the cabbage is just tender but still crunchy, season and then serve it in a warmed serving dish.

Almond Broccoli

Serves 6
Preparation: 8 mins
Cooking: 8 mins

1 cup sliced almonds
2 lb broccoli
3 tbsp butter
2 tbsp olive oil
1½ tbsp Japanese rice vinegar
sea salt and freshly ground black pepper

Place the almonds in a heavy-bottomed pan, sprinkle with salt and pepper, and dry roast over a moderate heat, moving them constantly to avoid burning. When the almonds are golden brown all over, remove them from the pan.

Wash the broccoli and trim it so that the florets and stems are all about the same size and shape.

Melt the butter with the olive oil in a pan over a moderate heat and mix in the rice vinegar. Add the broccoli and stir to coat with the mixture.

Increase the heat to high and stir-fry for 2 minutes. Reduce the heat to low, place the lid on the pan, and cook gently for about 3 minutes. Shake the pan vigorously from time to time to prevent the broccoli from sticking.

Remove the pan from the heat, transfer the broccoli to a warmed serving dish, sprinkle with the almonds, and serve.

Noodles

WITH PRIMROSE LEAVES

Please do not pick the increasingly rare wild primrose. A moist, steady, and cool spot in your own garden will allow you to cultivate this sweetly-scented flower. Swiss chard could also be substituted for the primrose leaves in this recipe.

Serves 4
Preparation: about 15 mins,
plus 30 mins resting
Cooking: about 10 mins

6 tbsp finely chopped primrose leaves
1¾ cups unbleached all-purpose flour
1 tsp salt
2 eggs
1½ tsp good quality corn oil
4 tbsp butter
10 primrose heads, for garnish
6 dry primrose leaves, for garnish

Steam the primrose leaves over boiling water for about 4 minutes, or until tender. Squeeze dry, then chop finely.

Place the flour mixed with half the salt on a cold marble board or work surface. Make a well in the center and put the eggs and 1 teaspoon of the corn oil in it. Using the fingers, gradually mix in the flour from the edges. When almost completely blended, add the chopped primrose leaves, distributing them evenly throughout the dough.

Knead the dough for 3 minutes, then roll into a ball. Rest for 30 minutes, covered with a damp cloth.

Divide the ball of dough into 4. Roll out one piece very thinly on a floured board (or use a pasta machine). Using a noodle cutter, if you have one, cut the pastry into noodles about ⅛-inch wide. Otherwise, roll up half the sheet toward the center like a Swiss roll; then roll up the other half to meet in the middle. With a very sharp knife cut into about ⅛-inch widths. Make noodles in the same way with the other 3 pieces of dough.

Bring to a boil a large pan of water to which has been added the remaining salt and corn oil (to prevent the noodles sticking). Add the noodles and cook for 3-5 minutes, until tender. Drain and toss with the butter and seasoning to taste. Garnish with the primrose flowers and leaves and eat quickly!

Hedgehog Potatoes

Serves 6 as an accompaniment or first
course, or 3 as a main course
Preparation: 15 mins
Cooking: 55-60 mins

12 medium-sized potatoes
2 tbsp sesame oil
sea salt and freshly ground black pepper
2 tbsp sesame seeds, toasted

Preheat the oven to 350°F.

Wash the potatoes well. Slice the potatoes thinly (about the thickness of a coin), but do not cut all the way down to the base.

Gently fan the slices open as much as possible without breaking them and put the potatoes in a roasting pan. Drizzle the sesame oil into the cuts and sprinkle with salt and pepper, then dust with the sesame seeds.

Bake on the middle shelf of the oven for 45 minutes or until tender, then raise the heat to 400°F and bake for a further 10-15 minutes, or until golden brown across the top (the surface of the potatoes should be crackly).

Serve immediately, covered with any seeds and oil from the pan.

Tenerife Potatoes

WITH HERB SAUCE

The herb sauce can be made in advance and refrigerated. It is useful for adding to vinaigrettes and is good on pasta dishes.

Serves 6-8 as an accompaniment
or 4 as a main course
Preparation: 10 mins
Cooking: about 20 mins

3 lb high quality medium-sized
new potatoes
1 tbsp kosher salt

for the herb sauce:
large bunch of fresh coriander (cilantro)
8 large garlic cloves, peeled
1½ tbsp white wine vinegar
2 heaping tsp Dijon mustard
1¼ cups extra virgin olive oil
salt and pepper

Wash the potatoes carefully, leaving all the skins on.

Bring a large pan of water to a boil and add the kosher salt. Add the potatoes, reduce the heat, and simmer until tender.

Remove the potatoes from the pan and cover, letting the salt dry on the skins.

Meanwhile, make the sauce: wash the coriander thoroughly and combine it (stems included) with the garlic, vinegar, and mustard in a blender. Pulse to mix well, and then gradually add the oil in a thin stream while the machine is running, to produce a sauce with a light, creamy consistency. Season with pepper and, sparingly, with salt (the salt on the potatoes should suffice).

Place a pool of sauce on the center of each of the plates and arrange the potatoes around the edge of the sauce.

Leeks Vinaigrette

Serves 6-8

Preparation: 15 mins

*Cooking: 12-20 mins, plus 2 or 3 hrs cooling
and chilling*

*8 medium leeks, trimmed, cleaned, and cut
across in half*

2 cups vegetable stock

*⅔ cup tarragon vinegar or Japanese rice
vinegar*

⅔ cup olive oil

*½ large green sweet pepper, seeded and
finely chopped*

*1 3-oz can of red pimientos, drained and
diced*

1 tsp sugar (optional)

1 tsp Dijon mustard

salt and pepper

shredded lettuce leaves, to serve

Take the root halves of the leeks and cut
them in half again lengthwise. Rinse all
the leeks again under cold running water.

Bring the stock to a boil in a pan and
drop the leeks into it. Simmer the leeks
for 8-15 minutes, until just tender but
still crisp. Remove from the stock and
drain thoroughly. Leave to cool.

Meanwhile, make the vinaigrette by
mixing the vinegar and oil together with
the sweet pepper, pimientos, sugar,
mustard, and salt and pepper to taste.

Once cool, place the leeks in a single
layer in a shallow flat-sided serving dish.
Mix the vinaigrette well and pour it over
the leeks. Cover and chill for several
hours, turning the leeks periodically.

To serve: transfer the leeks to a serving
plate dressed with lettuce leaves and
spoon the vinaigrette over the top.

Leeks Vinaigrette LEFT, *Tenerife Potatoes with
Herb Sauce* RIGHT (p. 33)

FISH AND SHELLFISH

Poached Haddock

WITH CAPERS

Serves 6
Preparation: 5 mins
Cooking: about 10 mins

2 lb smoked haddock (finnan haddie),
skinned
1¼ cups milk
2 tbsp butter
freshly ground black pepper
12 muffins, halved and buttered, to serve
(see page 26)
1 small jar of capers, drained

Place the haddock in a deep pan and cover with the milk. Put the lid on the pan, bring just to a boil, and simmer gently for about 8 minutes, or until the fish is thoroughly cooked (opaque and flakes readily when forked).

Remove the fish from the liquid and flake the flesh into a warm dish, removing any small bones and skin. Add the butter and some freshly ground black pepper. Then add just enough of the cooking liquid to bind the mixture together.

To serve: top the muffins with the fish mixture, then arrange 4 or 5 capers in a tight circle in the middle of each and serve hot.

Kipper Fillets

MARINATED IN LEMON
AND LIME

This dish benefits from long marination – up to 3 days is quite acceptable. It works equally well with herrings and is good served as a first course with toast or Scottish oatcakes.

Serves 8
Preparation: 20 mins
Marinating: at least 36 hrs

8 large kipper fillets, skinned and cut into
¼-inch wide strips
2 unwaxed lemons
2 unwaxed limes
1 cup olive oil
⅓ cup white wine vinegar
1 tsp Dijon mustard
salt and pepper

Place half the kippers side by side in a large flat dish to cover the bottom. Squeeze the juice of 1 lemon and 1 lime over the fish.

Make another layer of the remaining kipper fillets, then grate the peel and squeeze the juices of the remaining lemon and lime over this layer.

Make a vinaigrette with the oil, vinegar, mustard, and salt and pepper to taste. Pour this over the fish, cover, and chill for 24 hours.

Remove the cover, toss the fillets to bring those from the bottom to the top, and then flatten them down again. Cover and chill for a further 12 hours.

Seafood Soup

This soup is even.more delicious made the day before, adding the shellfish just before serving.

Serves 6 as a main course
Preparation: 30 mins, preferably
24 hrs ahead
Cooking: about 45 mins

2 lb fillets of smoked fish (cod or finnan
haddie)
5 cups milk
4 tbsp butter
2 tbsp vegetable oil
2 large onions, peeled and coarsely chopped
1 lb mealy potatoes, peeled and cut into
chunks
1 tsp grated nutmeg
salt and pepper
¾ lb small fresh, cooked, peeled shrimp,
washed
1½ lb small mussels, scrubbed
chopped parsley, for garnish
cream, to serve (optional)

Clean the fish fillets under running water. Put the milk with 2½ cups water in a pan and poach the fish gently in this, covered, for 15 minutes. Remove the fish from the milk and allow to cool. When cool enough to handle, flake the flesh carefully, removing any skin and bones. Reserve the cooking liquid.

Melt the butter with the oil in a large saucepan over a moderate heat. Add the onions and sauté until they are translucent. Add the potatoes, season well,

and allow to cook gently for 5 minutes.

Add the reserved cooking liquid and simmer for 15 minutes. Allow to cool a little, then pureé in a blender. Return the soup to the heat and add the flaked fish. Add the nutmeg and adjust the seasoning if necessary.

Add the shrimp and mussels to the soup 1 or 2 minutes before serving. Allow to heat through but do *not* let the soup boil.

Serve the soup in hot bowls, garnished with chopped parsley and swirls of cream if wished.

SAILING BY (*above*)
*A miniature antique sailing boat
evoke thoughts of the sea.*

Seafood Soup LEFT, *Scallops with
Lime Sauce* RIGHT *(p. 39) (overleaf)*

Scallops

Serves 6
Preparation: 15 mins
Cooking: 15 mins

12 large sea scallops
3 tbsp butter
1 onion, peeled and finely chopped
1¼ cups milk
salt and pepper

for the sauce:
yolks of 4 extra large eggs
3 tbsp butter
4 tsp grated lime peel (about 2 or 3 small
unwaxed limes)
⅔ cup sour cream
2 tsp lime juice

Clean and trim the scallops by removing the black vein and any remaining muscle. Rinse in cold water and pat dry.

First make the sauce. Mix the egg yolks, butter, and half the lime peel in the top of a double boiler and whisk over hot water until the butter has melted.

Gradually whisk in the sour cream until the sauce thickens slightly, then whisk in the lime juice. Season to taste and keep warm.

To cook the scallops, melt the butter in a skillet over a low heat and cook the onion in it until translucent.

Add the scallops, cover with the milk, and simmer gently for about 2-3 minutes, until the scallops are just poached (firm and opaque). Do not over-cook or they will become rubbery.

Remove from the pan and serve in warmed, scrubbed scallop shells or dishes with the lime sauce poured over and garnished with the remaining peel.

MEAT AND POULTRY

Paupiettes of Beef

WITH RED SAUCE

Serves 4-6
Preparation: 30 mins
Cooking: about 70-80 mins

2 tbsp butter
1 tbsp olive oil
2 large garlic cloves, peeled and chopped
2 shallots, peeled and chopped
¼ lb Canadian bacon, finely chopped
¼ lb (about 1 cup) cooked chicken meat, finely chopped
2 cups fresh brown bread crumbs
1½ tbsp chopped fresh parsley
1 tsp chopped fresh or ½ tsp dried marjoram
salt and pepper
1 extra large egg, lightly beaten
⅓ cup cognac
1½ lb lean beef top round, sliced wafer thin
1 heaping tbsp Dijon mustard
chopped parsley, for garnish
scallion greens, cut into 1-inch long strips, for garnish

for the sauce:
2 tbsp olive oil
2 garlic cloves, peeled and chopped
8 scallions, including green stems, chopped
2 large red sweet peppers, seeded and finely chopped
pinch of chili powder
pinch of cayenne
2 tbsp dry sherry
1¼ cups vegetable stock

Preheat the oven to 325°F.

Melt the butter with the oil in a shallow flameproof casserole over a moderate heat. Add the garlic and shallot and cook gently until soft and translucent.

Meanwhile in a mixing bowl, combine the bacon, chicken, bread crumbs, parsley, marjoram, and salt and pepper to taste. Add the egg and mix well to bind, then add the cognac. Cover.

The slices of beef should measure roughly 3 x 3 inches. If necessary, put them between sheets of waxed paper and beat thinner with a rolling pin or meat pounder. Spread each slice with mustard and season well. Spoon stuffing equally over each slice. Roll up the slices neatly, tucking in the ends to contain the stuffing. Tie each paupiette carefully with string.

Place the paupiettes in the casserole with the garlic and shallot, and over a moderate to high heat brown them all over. Cover and cook in the oven for 50 minutes. Remove the lid, increase the oven temperature to 400°F, and cook for a further 5 minutes. Turn the paupiettes at least twice during the cooking.

Meanwhile, make the sauce: heat the oil in a heavy-bottomed saucepan over a moderate heat and cook the garlic, scallions, and sweet peppers until soft and tender.

Stir in the chili powder, cayenne, and salt to taste and cook for a further 1 minute. Add the liquids and bring to a boil, then simmer to reduce the sauce slightly. Cool.

Purée the sauce in a blender, then strain through a fine sieve into a clean pan and warm through gently. Take the strings off the cooked paupiettes, put them on a warmed serving dish, and coat with the sauce. Garnish and serve.

Seared Lamb Slices

WITH LEMON THYME

Serves 6
Preparation: 10 mins
Cooking: about 5 mins

12 sprigs of lemon thyme
1 tbsp olive oil
4 tbsp butter
1½ lb boneless loin of lamb from a rack, sliced into ¼-inch thick disks
1 tbsp lemon pepper
salt and pepper

Put 8 of the thyme sprigs in a heatproof bowl and pour 1 cup of boiling water over them. Leave the thyme to infuse for a few minutes. Roughly chop the remaining sprigs.

Heat a ridged grill pan over a high heat and put half of the oil and butter on the pan. (Do not allow the fats to burn!) Place the lamb pieces on the pan so that they sear as they touch and leave to cook for about 1 minute. Turn and cook similarly on the other side. (The meat should stay quite pink on the inside.) Transfer the lamb to a warmed serving dish and keep warm.

Add the rest of the oil and butter to the fats already in the pan along with the lemon pepper. Slowly increase the heat and gradually add the thyme infusion, including the leaves.

Allow to bubble, adding salt and pepper to taste, then quickly pour the sauce, including the thyme sprigs, over the meat. Sprinkle the chopped thyme over the top and serve immediately.

CLOTH OF GOLD
Sunny rape flowers swathe the fields as far as the eye can see.

Deviled Kidneys

The perfect hearty breakfast!

Serves 6
Preparation: 15 mins
Cooking: about 15 mins

12 lamb kidneys
2 tbsp butter
2 tbsp corn oil
1 large onion, peeled and diced
¼ lb flat mushrooms, wiped and chopped
2 tsp Dijon mustard
1 tsp mushroom ketchup
4 tsp Worcestershire sauce
¼ tsp cayenne
sea salt and black pepper

Halve the kidneys, removing any membranes and the white cores. Rinse and pat dry.

Heat half the butter with the oil in a skillet over a moderate heat and gently fry the kidney halves for about 4 minutes on each side. Remove the kidneys from the pan, transfer to a warmed flameproof dish and keep warm.

Place the onion in the pan and cook gently in the juices until softened, then add the mushrooms. Stir until cooked. Add the remaining butter and allow it to melt, then add the mustard, ketchup, and Worcestershire sauce, stirring everything all the time.

Preheat the broiler.

Raise the heat slightly under the mushroom mixture, then add the cayenne and salt and pepper to taste, mixing it thoroughly. Add enough water to make a sauce. Allow this sauce to bubble for about 30 seconds, then pour it over the kidneys and broil for about 1 minute.

Serve immediately with toast.

Chicken

WITH COCONUT AND LEMON

Serves 6-8
Preparation: 15 mins
Cooking: 15-20 min per pound plus
about 10 mins

4 unwaxed lemons
1 fresh chicken, dressed weight about 5 lb
1 4½-oz can of coconut milk
6 tbsp butter, softened
salt and pepper

Preheat the oven to 400°F.

Quarter 3 of the lemons. Rinse out the cavity of the chicken and drain well. Stuff loosely with the lemon quarters and place the bird in a roasting pan.

Using the blunt rounded handle of a spoon, gently pull back the skin over each breast half without puncturing it. Spread the thick, paste-like part of the coconut milk evenly over the breast. Lay the skin back in place.

Spread the butter over the entire breast down to the legs. Season the bird well all over. Fill the cavity with the remaining coconut milk, then stuff the end with the whole lemon, skin side out.

Pour ⅔ cup of water into the pan and roast the bird for 15-20 minutes per pound, basting from time to time.

Twenty minutes before the end of cooking time, keeping the bird in the pan, squash the lemons inside the cavity with the back end of a spoon to release the juices. Gently raise the bird and empty most of the cavity juices into the juices in the pan. If the bird is not sufficiently browned, turn the heat up slightly for the final period of cooking.

Take the chicken out of the pan. Remove and discard the lemons from the bird, squashing again to release any juices into the sauce. Carefully empty the cavity juices into the roasting pan. Place the bird on a warmed serving dish.

Place the roasting pan over a high heat and bring the sauce to a boil. Adjust the seasoning and add more butter or water as necessary. Carve the bird and serve the sauce separately.

Chicken with Coconut and Lemon (left)

CLOUDS OF CHERVIL *(above)*

Summer

SEASON OF THE SENSES

Summer is the season when the living community functions at its fullest: vegetation supports a huge number and great diversity of animals, birds, and insects and with summer's fruit and flowers, leaves and roots, sap and bark there is an abundance of food for the busy raising of the young. The fields and hedgerows are literally blooming, overflowing with colors and smells. Take children for rambles through meadows full of clover; search for ladybugs and spiders, and explain how they aid the farmer in controlling aphids, bugs, and beetles that would otherwise chomp their way through crops at an alarming rate; and revel with them in their childish delight at the wonders that surround them in this season at every glance and every step.

RESTING AMONG THE HERBS (*above*)

SUMMER ABUNDANCE (*previous page*)

From June to September, you can go badger-watching (make sure you are always downwind of the sett). Although shy, when they are unaware of a human presence these sturdy creatures are boisterous and mischievous in play, and with a long lens it's possible to take magical photographs.

In July and August, pick reeds and rushes to make rough baskets, wetting them before braiding and weaving. Encourage children to learn about bats that fly in the late-evening skies. These fascinating nocturnal mammals do great work in pest control, so if they do make a home on your patch, welcome them to stay. The timbers around their nesting area will be kept completely free of that devastating insect, the termite, which can be so destructive in homes with elderly timbers.

Crystallized Petals and Flowers

Quite a variety of flowers suit this treatment as they keep their color well: borage, lavender, marigold (calendula, *not* African Tagetes which is poisonous), rose and individual rose petals, violet, primrose, and daisy.

If the flowers need only last a few days: beat an egg white until frothy and sticky but not stiff. Paint the flowers and petals on all sides. Then immediately dust them with sugar and allow them to dry at room temperature until crisp. Store in an airtight container.

If the flowers have to last a few weeks: mix together 2 tablespoons of vodka or gin and 1 teaspoon of gum arabic, paint the flowers with this mixture, and dust well with sugar as described above. Shake off any surplus sugar and leave the flowers to dry until crisp. Store in an airtight container.

Flower and Petal Ice Bowl

Present the ice bowl on a tray or dish deep enough to accommodate extra flower heads that can be scattered over to float as the sculpture unfreezes. This takes about 1-2 hours depending on the room temperature.

Place 4-6 ice cubes in the bottom of a large freezerproof bowl, then place a smaller bowl (approximately one third smaller) into the large bowl, weighting it down to hold it in place. Pour ice water into the gap, and arrange flowers and foliage of your choice in the water, with their heads pointing outward. (You may need to use extra ice cubes to anchor them in place.) Fill up with extra ice water, if necessary, to come up to the rim of the bowl, then freeze until completely solid.

Remove from the freezer and leave at room temperature for about half an hour. The inner bowl should then come out quite easily. If it does not, dip the whole thing into warm water and wiggle the inner bowl until it becomes loose and you can remove the ice mold. Replace in the freezer until required.

Blueberries can be dried now and kept for making blueberry vinegar in winter (see page 106). A rewarding project in which children can join is crystallizing flower heads and petals. They look quite beautiful, taste good, and jazz up all sorts of cakes and desserts. Iced petals and flowers are fun to make into a centerpiece.

Picnics can be such fun and, when food is prepared in advance, little trouble to pack. Mousses and terrines, tarts and cold soups make delicious picnics to enjoy while watching baseball or other sports, or when fishing or at a fair. Keep in mind color and texture, as well as taste, when deciding on the menu and your picnic will resemble a feast. In these days of the thermos, ice chest, and lightweight picnic equipment, a wonderfully relaxed day in the summer sunshine can be guaranteed.

Go mad with salads while so much is available from our fertile soil. Combine exotic fruits with grilled goat's cheese and make warm oil vinaigrettes; watercress, beetroot, and tangerine combine well in a salad, and for garnishes and dressings you can be generous with fresh herbs, which also promote health in a delicious way.

If guests become weary from all the activity, the change of air, or a simple indulgence in good plain food, give them parsley honey at bed-time and they will quickly be restored. This natural restorative can be made by anyone with an ample supply of parsley from their garden or window box.

Make elderflower champagne (see page 52), in which the scent of the flowers still comes through. Boil camomile flowers in water, then strain and use the liquid to rinse your hair after a shampoo. Its natural dye adds luster to blonde hair, as do hops, which can be used in the same way for a rinse for brunettes.

Use the extraordinary, bright blue flowers of borage to dress cakes and salads. Wild dog rose petals are particularly good for this purpose, too, as they have dark edges graduating to pale pink centers. Comfrey, quickly blanched, can be applied to bruises and bandaged on overnight. You will be amazed at how quickly the bruising will go down. Pick hedgerow weeds to make lovely floral displays, both large and small. A posy of buttercups and chervil can be quite simply exquisite. Mallow and meadowsweet interspersed with any of the fresh mints make a lovely smelling vase to place in guests' bedrooms. Roses, of course, find their way into homes everywhere in this season. Sweet-scented sweetpeas with their vibrant hues create fine splashes of color, and the wonderfully frail-looking poppy amid the golden, ripening corn remains one of the eternal sights of summer.

Outdoor theater and the much-loved barbecue, the beach and the river bank are places to enjoy during the gentle weather of this season. Sunshine soothes the soul and makes people more sociable, and painting and poetry, weaving and writing can be indulged in while soaking up the atmosphere of the countryside and inhaling fresh air.

Parsley Honey

Parsley is a most valuable and versatile herb and has marvelous healing powers. This honey can simply be eaten to enliven tired minds and bodies, or it may also be used as an alternative to more usual table condiments.

Fills three 1-lb jars

4 oz fresh parsley, chopped (about 2 cups)
2 lb (4½ cups) sugar

Put the chopped parsley into a pan with 1 quart hot water and leave to infuse for 20 minutes, then bring the water to a boil. The color should drain from the parsley into the water.

Immediately strain off the liquid and add the sugar. Return the liquid to a moderate heat to dissolve the sugar, stirring constantly, then bring to a boil and continue to boil until the liquid starts to thicken.

Remove from the heat and pour into warm, dry, sterilized, screw-topped glass jars. Seal and label.

PAINTERLY COLOR
Nature competes with art in this splash of summer red against a richly painted canvas.

THE SEASON'S RICHES *(overleaf)*
The vegetable and fruit gardens overflow with ripe, delicious produce.

MENUS *for Summer*

PREPARATION

Elderflower Champagne

Makes about 4½ quarts
Preparation: 10 mins
Cooking: about 25 mins, 10 days ahead

8 large flowering heads of elder
4½ quarts spring water or filtered
tap water
3 cups sugar
2 unwaxed lemons, sliced and seeds
removed
2 tbsp white wine vinegar

Shake the elderflower heads well to rid them of any clinging insects. Rinse and pat the flowers dry with paper towels.

In a large pan, bring the water to a boil and remove from the heat once boiling. Immediately dissolve the sugar in the water, stirring constantly. Leave to cool.

When completely cold, add the flower heads, lemon slices, and vinegar. Leave for 48 hours.

At the end of this time, strain the liquid carefully through cheesecloth, then transfer to dry, sterilized, long-necked, clear glass bottles with corks.

As with real champagne, the contents of the bottles can become very lively, so it is recommended that the corks be wired for safety.

The elderflower champagne is ready to drink after 8 days. Serve well chilled as a fizzy, heady, and delicious aperitif.

Garlic and Herb Bread

Makes two large (or four small) loaves
Preparation: 15 mins plus 30 mins proving
Cooking: 40-50 mins, plus cooling

3 lb (12 cups) wholewheat flour
1 tbsp fine sea salt
¼ cup chopped fresh oregano
4 tsp chopped fresh young rosemary
2 tsp chopped fresh thyme
1½ tsp ground turmeric
24 garlic cloves, peeled and chopped
1 large onion, peeled and diced (optional)
1 oz compressed yeast
1 tbsp raw cane sugar

Put the flour into a large mixing bowl and mix in the salt, herbs, turmeric, garlic, and onion, if using.

Into ½ cup of lukewarm water, crumble the yeast along with the sugar. Leave for 10-15 minutes in a warm place until the mixture becomes frothy.

Pour the yeast mixture slowly into the flour mixture and gradually incorporate a further 2½ cups lukewarm water. Using the hands, mix the ingredients together thoroughly, then divide the dough into 2 equal balls.

Grease two 9 x 5 x 3-inch loaf pans with a little butter or oil. Slightly warm the 2 prepared loaf pans, then place a ball of dough in each. Cover each with a dampened dish towel, place in a warm spot, and allow to rise until just above the rim of the pan.

Preheat the oven to 400°F.

Quickly put the prepared loaves in the oven and bake for about 40 minutes, until the loaves sound hollow when their bases are tapped.

Gently loosen the sides of the loaves from the pans and leave to cool a little, then unmold them onto a wire rack to cool completely.

Croissants

Makes 12
Preparation: 2 hrs, plus chilling
Cooking: 20 mins

3¼ cups bread flour, sifted
2 tbsp shortening
2 tsp salt
1 oz compressed yeast
2 eggs
1½ sticks butter
½ tsp sugar

Place the flour in a large bowl with the shortening and rub the shortening into the flour with the fingertips until the mixture looks like large bread crumbs. Add the salt, mix together, and make a well in the center.

Cream the yeast in 1¼ cups lukewarm water with a fork until frothy, then add this to the well along with one of the eggs. Using the fingertips again, blend in the flour, then beat the dough until it leaves the sides of the bowl cleanly.

Put the dough on a lightly floured cool surface and knead it for about 10 minutes until smooth.

With a wooden spoon soften the butter slightly, until it is pliable and creamy but not too soft, then divide it into 3 roughly equal portions.

Roll out the dough into a rectangle about 20 x 8 inches, which is about ¼-inch thick. Trim, if necessary.

Dot one portion of the butter over two-thirds of the length of the dough, also leaving a ½-inch border around all the edges. Fold the dough in three, bringing up and in the unbuttered one-third first and then folding in the opposite third. Turn the dough a quarter turn and then seal the edges by pressing them with the rolling pin.

Again pressing with the rolling pin, shape the dough into a long strip and roll into a rectangle as before. Repeat the process of dotting with butter, folding in, and turning the dough. Repeat this entire process for a third time. At all times try to keep the corners of the dough square and the edges straight.

Wrap the dough in a dampened dish towel and chill for 45 minutes.

Repeat the rolling and folding process 3 more times (although *not* dotting with butter), turning a quarter turn each time and allowing the dough to rest and chill wrapped in the towel for 45 minutes between each process.

After a final chilling, roll out the dough on a lightly floured surface into a rectangle about 25 x 13 inches. Cover again and leave to rest at room temperature for 10 minutes.

Cut the dough in half and trim into two 12-inch squares. Cut each of these in half and then cut the halves into 3 triangles with 6-inch bases.

In a small bowl, place the other egg and beat it lightly, then add the sugar and about 6 drops of water. Mix together well. Using a pastry bush, paint the pastry triangles with the egg wash.

Loosely roll up the triangles from the bases. Leaving the tip of the triangle on the underside, carefully curve them into crescent shapes.

Place the croissants on a baking sheet and glaze them lightly again with the egg wash. Cover with waxed paper and leave to rise for about 40 minutes at room temperature.

Preheat the oven to 425°F.

At the end of the rising time, give the croissants another quick coating of egg wash, then place the baking sheet in the middle of the oven and bake for 17-20 minutes, until golden brown.

Ease the cooked croissants from the sheet using a spatula if necessary. Allow them to cool slightly on a wire rack before serving or filling (see page 64 for suggestions).

Scones

Makes 12
Preparation: 15 mins
Cooking: 10-12 mins

4 tbsp butter
¾ cup sour cream
(or equal parts sour cream and milk)
1 egg
2 cups self-rising flour, sifted
pinch of salt
1 egg yolk, beaten (optional)

Preheat the oven to 450°F and lightly grease a baking sheet with a little butter.

Melt the butter gently in a small pan over a low heat, then add to the sour cream (or cream and milk mixture) along with the egg. Stir in the flour and salt and mix to a smooth dough.

Turn out the dough onto a lightly floured surface which is as cold as possible (marble is ideal) and knead lightly for about 2 minutes.

Pat the dough flat with the palm of the hand until it is about ¾-in thick. Using a 2-inch round cookie cutter, cut the dough into rounds. Place these on the prepared baking sheet, brush with beaten egg yolk, if wished, and bake for about 10-12 minutes until golden brown.

Japonica Jam

Japonica quinces, slightly larger than crab apples and a pale golden color, make beautiful jam with a distinctive flavor.

Makes about 4 lb
Preparation: 10 mins
Cooking: 30 mins, plus cooling

4 lb Japonica quinces
sugar
1 heaping tsp ground cloves

Wash the fruit and chop it into rough chunks. Place these in a pan with 5 pints water. Bring to a boil, then allow to boil gently until the flesh is tender. Allow to cool and then press through a sieve.

Weigh the resulting pulp and add an equal weight of sugar. Return to the pan and bring to a boil again, stirring constantly. Add the cloves and continue to boil.

After about 10 minutes boiling, start testing for a gel point (see Chunky Seville Marmalade, page 24).

When it is ready, pour the jam into warmed, dry, sterilized glass jars and seal immediately with screw-tops or disks of waxed paper, cellophane, and rubber bands as for Chunky Seville Marmalade.

Melting Moments

WITH CHOCOLATE COATING

You can omit the chocolate if you would just like plain cookies.

Makes about 40
Preparation: 20 mins
Cooking: 15 mins, plus cooling and decorating

½ cup confectioners' sugar, sifted
2 sticks butter, softened
½ cup cornstarch
1¼ cup all-purpose flour
2 tbsp shortening
2 tsp grated peel from an unwaxed orange
8 oz semisweet chocolate (or equal parts semisweet and milk chocolate)

Preheat the oven to 350°F and lightly grease a baking sheet with a little butter.

Cream the confectioners' sugar with the butter in a bowl until the mixture is light and fluffy. Gradually add the cornstarch and then the flour, mixing thoroughly.

Put the mixture into a decorating bag fitted with a large fluted tube and pipe small stars of the dough on the prepared baking sheet. Bake for about 10-15 minutes, until golden brown. Cool on a wire rack.

Place the shortening, grated peel, and chocolate in a bowl and warm in a bain-marie. Mix well until thoroughly melted.

Dip one half of each cookie into the chocolate mixture. Alternatively, paint it on with a brush, making a decorative shape in the middle, or paint a ½-inch rim around the edge, etc.

DAPPLED LIGHT
The warmth of summer sunshine permeates every nook and cranny.

CHILLED SOUPS

Chilled Lebanese Soup

This and the three chilled soups which follow are ideal for making a day ahead as they all benefit from long chilling. This wonderfully refreshing cucumber and yogurt soup is like a liquid salad.

Serves 6
Preparation: 20 mins, 24 hrs ahead

2 large English cucumbers (with green, unblemished skins)
2 tbsp tarragon vinegar
2 garlic cloves, peeled and minced
½ cup thick unflavored yogurt
½ cup light cream
1¼ cups strong vegetable stock, cold
1 tbsp finely chopped gherkin or cornichon
1 red onion, peeled and diced
¼ lb small peeled cooked shrimp
salt and pepper
2 tbsp chopped parsley, for garnish

Wash the cucumbers, pat them dry, and grate them coarsely into a large mixing bowl. Add the vinegar and garlic and stir in the yogurt, followed by the cream and then the stock.

Season well and mix in the gherkin and onion. Chill in the refrigerator overnight. Just before serving, stir in the shrimp, check seasoning and sprinkle over the chopped parsley.

Watercress Soup

This soup is equally delicious served chilled or hot.

Serves 8
Preparation: 10 mins
Cooking: 35 mins, 24 hrs ahead

2 large bunches of watercress
2 cups vegetable stock
3 tbsp butter
1 large onion, peeled and chopped
3 tbsp flour
1¼ cups milk
1 heaping tsp Dijon mustard
1½ tsp tarragon vinegar
1¼ cups light cream
salt and pepper

Wash the watercress thoroughly and cut it up, with the stems, reserving the best leaves for garnish.

Put half of the watercress in a pan with the stock and 1¼ cups water. Bring to a boil, then reduce the heat and simmer gently for 20 minutes. Remove from the heat and allow to cool.

Melt the butter in a pan and add the remaining watercress. Sauté gently for 5 minutes, then add the onion and cook for about 5 minutes more.

Stir in the flour, then gradually add the milk, stirring constantly to make a smooth sauce. Simmer for a minute or two, then add the mustard and vinegar. Allow to cool.

Combine both watercress mixtures and purée in a blender. Add the cream, season well, and keep in the refrigerator until well chilled.

Serve the chilled soup garnished with the reserved watercress leaves.

Rich Minted Yogurt Soup

Fresh mint leaves add tanginess to cream and thick yogurt. Use common garden or lemon mint if possible.

Serves 6
Preparation: 5 mins, 24 hrs ahead

2½ cups thick unflavored yogurt
1¼ cups light cream
½ tsp toasted cumin, ground
2 cups vegetable stock
1 tsp lemon juice
1 tsp lime juice
salt and pepper
about 12 leaves of fresh mint

Lightly whisk the yogurt with a fork until smooth. Gradually whisk in the cream, cumin, stock, and lemon and lime juices. Season well, then store the soup in the refrigerator until well chilled.

Just before serving, place the mint leaves on top of each other, roll them up, and snip into fine shreds. Sprinkle these on the soup to garnish.

Chilled Apricot Soup

Serves 8
Preparation: 20 mins, 24 hrs ahead

½ lb dried apricots
¾ lb fresh apricots, pitted
½ cup sugar
2 pints dry white wine
juice and grated peel of ½
unwaxed lemon
juice and grated peel of ½ unwaxed lime
1¼ cups light cream, chilled
finely chopped parsley, for garnish

Choose plump and juicy dried apricots and reserve the 8 best-looking halves. Pour boiling water over the others to cover and leave to soak until soft. Discard the water and rinse the apricots in cold water.

Combine the fresh and rinsed dried apricots and in a blender purée them well to a fine pulp.

Dissolve the sugar in the white wine and add this to the apricot pulp. Blend again, then add the lemon and lime juices and peel. Store in the refrigerator until well chilled.

Swirl the cream into the soup and serve garnished with the parsley and the reserved apricots sliced very thinly.

Rich Minted Yogurt Soup LEFT *(p. 55),*
Watercress Soup CENTRE *(p. 55),*
Chilled Apricot Soup RIGHT

VEGETABLES AND HERBS

Asparagus Tartlets

Makes 16 tartlets
Preparation: 20 mins
Cooking: about 20 mins

1²⁄₃ cups all-purpose flour, sifted
½ tsp salt
10 tbsp butter, softened
¾ lb thin young asparagus spears, trimmed
8 eggs
²⁄₃ cup heavy cream
salt
½ tsp freshly ground black pepper

Preheat the oven to 400°F and lightly grease sixteen 3-inch tartlet molds with a little butter.

Make the pastry: mix the flour with the salt in a bowl, then rub in 8 tablespoons (1 stick) of the butter until the mixture has the consistency of fine bread crumbs.

Stir in enough ice water to make a soft, but not sticky, dough and roll this out on a floured surface to a thickness of about ⅛ inch. Cut out 16 rounds of dough big enough to line the tartlet molds.

Prick the pastry cases all over, line with rounds of baking parchment, and weight with dried beans. Bake for 10 minutes. Remove the beans and paper and bake for a further 5 minutes until the pastry is light golden in color.

Meanwhile, make the filling: steam the asparagus until just tender. Remove and reserve 32 good-looking tips. Mash the remaining asparagus and warm gently in a dry pan.

Beat the eggs well, then mix in the cream. Season well with salt and the freshly ground black pepper.

Melt the remaining butter in a heavy-bottomed pan and add the egg mixture. Cook over a gentle heat, stirring constantly, until the mixture is just beginning to set but is still quite creamy. Mix in the warmed asparagus and beat well with a wooden spoon.

Spoon the filling into the pastry cases, garnish each with 2 of the reserved asparagus tips, crossed, and serve.

Note: the pastry cases may be made ahead and stored in an airtight container until they are needed. Warm them through in a low oven before filling.

Herbed New Potatoes

Serves 6
Preparation: 15 mins
Cooking: about 20 mins

2 lb new potatoes
1 cup chopped fresh parsley
½ cup chopped fresh chives
½ cup chopped fresh coriander (cilantro)
6 tbsp butter
salt and pepper

Scrub the potatoes well, then plunge them into a large pan of boiling salted water. Cook for about 20 minutes, or until tender. Drain and keep warm.

Mix the herbs. Melt the butter in the bottom of a warmed serving dish and scatter the herbs on top. Add the potatoes, season well, and toss until they are all covered with the herb butter.

Green Beans

WITH CAPER LEAF
VINAIGRETTE

Serves 4-6
Preparation: 15 mins
Cooking: 5 mins

1 4-oz can caper leaves, drained
1½ lb fine young green beans, trimmed
kosher salt
4 tbsp virgin olive oil
1 tbsp Japanese rice vinegar
1 tbsp crème fraîche
2 heaping tsp Dijon mustard
1 tbsp finely chopped capers
2 or 3 tbsp milk
salt and pepper

Carefully pick the caper leaves off the stems. Discard the thorny stems and chop the leaves roughly.

Add some kosher salt to a large pan of water, bring to a boil, and plunge the beans into it. Stir for about 4 minutes, then drain the beans and refresh briefly under cold running water. Place in a warmed serving dish.

Mix together all the other ingredients with the caper leaves, using the milk to dilute to a good coating consistency if necessary. Season the sauce to taste and pour over the beans.

FIELDS OF GREEN (*above right*)
Lush pastures beckon to leisurely picnics.

Summer Vegetables

CRISPLY SAUTÉED

Serves 6
Preparation: 20 mins
Cooking: about 5 mins

2 bunches of scallions
3½ tbsp sesame oil
4 tbsp butter
1½ tbsp kosher salt
1 tsp freshly ground black pepper
3 tbsp finely grated unpeeled
fresh gingerroot

juice of 1 small lime
6 oz snow peas, trimmed and cut in half
lengthwise
¼ lb young carrots, cleaned and cut
into julienne strips
1½ large stalks of firm white celery,
trimmed and thinly sliced
¼ lb fine green beans, trimmed
½ cup pumpkin seeds, dry roasted
1 tbsp chopped mixed parsley and chives,
for garnish

Cut the green tops from the scallions and reserve. Slice the bulbs in half.

Heat the sesame oil and butter gently in a wok (or large sauté pan). Add the scallions and half each of the salt, pepper, ginger, and lime juice. Sauté gently until the scallions are slightly translucent but not completely soft.

Increase the heat and add all the vegetables. Stir and toss so that they are all well covered with the oil and butter mixture. Cook for 3-5 minutes, or until they are all tender but still firm.

Add the remaining salt, pepper, ginger, and lime juice. Toss in the pumpkin seeds and stir to mix well. Transfer to a warmed serving dish and garnish generously with the chopped herbs and snipped scallion tops.

Fava Beans

WITH PINE NUTS AND BASIL SAUCE

Serves 8
Preparation: 20 mins
Cooking: about 10 mins

3 tbsp butter
5 tbsp flour, sifted
2½ cups milk
1 tsp Dijon mustard

1½ tsp Japanese rice vinegar
3 heaping tbsp pesto sauce
8 lb young tender fava (broad) beans, shelled
1¼ cups pine nuts
10 basil leaves, snipped
salt and pepper

Melt the butter in a heavy-bottomed saucepan over a low heat. Add the flour and cook gently, stirring constantly, for about 3 minutes.

Remove the pan from the heat and gradually add one-third of the milk, whisking to combine it well. Return the pan to the heat and whisk as the mixture thickens. Repeat this process until all the milk has been incorporated. Add the mustard, rice vinegar, and pesto sauce, stirring gently to mix.

Cook the beans in lightly salted boiling water for 3 minutes. Drain and refresh briefly in cold water. Place in a warmed serving dish and cover with the pine nuts, reserving a few for garnish.

Pour the sauce over the beans and garnish with the snipped basil leaves and the reserved pine nuts.

FISH AND MEAT

Snow Peas

WITH SHRIMP AND
LUMPFISH CAVIAR

Serves 6
Preparation: 15 mins
Cooking: 5 mins

2 lb snow peas, trimmed
¾ lb small fresh (not frozen) peeled cooked
shrimp
1½ tbsp crème fraîche
2 sprigs of dill, for garnish
10 borage flower heads

for the vinaigrette:
3 tbsp oil
1 tbsp vinegar
2 heaping tsp Bordeaux mustard
juice of ½ lemon
½ tsp sugar
salt and pepper
1 4-oz jar black lumpfish caviar

Plunge the snow peas into a pan of lightly
salted boiling water and blanch for 2
minutes, stirring constantly. Drain and
refresh the peas briefly under cold
running water.

Place the peas in a glass serving dish or
bowl and sprinkle over the shrimp.

Summer Vegetables Crisply Sautéed LEFT
*(p.59), Fava Beans with Pine Nuts and Basil
Sauce* CENTRE, *Snow Peas with Shrimp
and Lumpfish Caviar* RIGHT

Make the vinaigrette using the oil,
vinegar, mustard, lemon juice, sugar, and
salt and pepper to taste. Stir in the
lumpfish caviar, reserving a little for
the garnish.

Just before serving, dress the peas and
shrimp with the vinaigrette and toss
gently. Place the crème fraîche on top in
the middle and garnish that with the
reserved caviar, dill, and some of the
borage. Sprinkle the remaining borage
petals over the salad and serve
immediately.

Note: if the salad is dressed too early,
the caviar will stain the shrimp.

Buckwheat Crêpes

WITH SMOKED EEL AND
SOUR CREAM

You could let guests help themselves
to the crêpe fillings.

Makes 20
Preparation: 15 mins, 2 hrs ahead
Cooking: about 40 mins

1 cup + 3 tbsp buckwheat flour
1 cup stoneground wholewheat flour
1 tsp salt
2 eggs, beaten
2½ cups low-fat milk
2 unwaxed lemons
2 unwaxed limes
2 bunches of scallions
1 cup sour cream
¾ lb smoked eel fillets, thinly sliced
vegetable oil, for frying

Place the flours in a mixing bowl with the
salt. Mix and create a well in the middle.
Put the eggs in the well.

Using a balloon whisk in a rotating
movement, gradually incorporate the
milk into the mixture, gathering in the
flours from the sides a little at a time until
the batter is smooth and has a good
pouring consistency (a little extra milk
may be needed). Leave to stand for at
least 2 hours.

Cut each lemon and lime into 12
wedges and reserve. Trim and clean the
scallions and slice them (including the
green leaves) into rings about ⅛-inch
thick. Place in a bowl. Put the sour cream
in a similar bowl.

Arrange the slices of smoked eel on a
large serving plate and garnish with the
lemon and lime wedges.

Heat a small quantity of oil in a crêpe
pan or small skillet over a moderate heat.
Pour in just enough batter to cover the
bottom with a thin layer, tilting and
swirling the pan as the batter goes in to
coat the bottom.

Cook the crêpe for a minute or so until
small bubbles appear on the surface, then
flip over and cook the other side. Turn
out of the pan onto a warmed serving
plate, cover with foil, and keep warm in a
low oven.

Cook all the crêpes in the same way
and stack on the serving plate in the
oven, with a sheet of kitchen paper
between each one.

When they are all cooked, serve with
the accompaniments. Encourage guests
to place some sour cream on a crêpe, top
this with a slice of eel and some scallions,
season to taste, squeeze over some lemon
or lime juice, and then roll up the crêpe
into a cylinder to eat it.

Halibut Steaks

WITH SAMPHIRE

Serves 6
Preparation: 5 mins
Cooking: about 35 mins

6 halibut steaks, each weighing about 6 oz
½ cup heavy cream
2 egg yolks
½ tsp cornstarch
6 tbsp Noilly Prat
juice of ½ lemon
juice of ½ lime
salt and pepper
2 lb fresh samphire or fine asparagus spears

Preheat the oven to 400°F and place the steaks in a lightly oiled ovenproof dish.

Put the cream, egg yolks, and cornstarch into a bain-marie or double boiler over gentle heat and stir constantly until the mixture thickens. Add the Noilly Prat, lemon and lime juices, and salt and pepper to taste.

Pour the sauce over the fish, cover with foil, and bake for 20 minutes. At the end of this time, remove the foil, increase the oven temperature to 425°F, and cook for a further 5 minutes. Remove the dish from the oven and keep hot.

Wash the samphire thoroughly, or trim asparagus, and toss into a large pan of *unsalted* boiling water. Cook, stirring frequently, for 2-3 minutes, then drain well and make nests of it on each of 6 warmed plates.

Place the halibut steaks in the center of each samphire or asparagus nest and serve the sauce separately.

Salmon

WITH FRESH GINGER AND
MUSTARD FLOWER SAUCE

If mustard flower heads are not available, use other flower heads or herbs for the garnish.

Serves 6
Preparation: 10 mins
Cooking: about 15 mins

6 fresh salmon steaks, each weighing
about 6 oz
salt and freshly ground black pepper
1 bottle (70 cl) dry white wine
1 tbsp grated peeled fresh gingerroot

for the sauce:
1¼ cups milk
2 tbsp mustard flower heads
1 tbsp butter
1 tsp English mustard powder
2 tbsp flour
½ tbsp white wine vinegar

First prepare the sauce ingredients: in a small pan, heat the milk almost to boiling point, and put the mustard flower heads into it, reserving 2 for garnish. Remove the pan from the heat and leave to infuse for 10 minutes.

Season the salmon with salt and black pepper. Put the wine into a pan with the ginger, bring to just below the boil, and add the fish. Cover and simmer very gently for about 8 minutes.

Meanwhile, finish the sauce: melt the butter in a heavy-bottomed pan over a low heat. Add the mustard powder and the flour. Cook for 3 minutes, stirring constantly. Stir in the vinegar. Gradually add the flower heads with the milk, then bring the mixture to a boil.

Season and keep warm.

Remove the fish from the wine and strain the ginger from the liquid (reserve or freeze this for use as a fish stock). Place the fish on a warm serving dish and sprinkle with the ginger.

Cover the fish with the sauce, garnish with the reserved flower heads, and serve immediately.

Croissant Fillings

Although it is usually associated with sweet things, virtually any filling and any combination – including sweet and savory ones – can be used for the versatile croissant (see page 52). Stuffed croissants make perfect breakfast or light supper dishes.

Fills 12 croissants
Preparation: 15 mins
Cooking: 10 mins

6 slices of country-style bacon
12 prunes, pitted
12 dried apricots, pitted
4 tbsp butter
2½ tbsp flour
¾ cup milk
salt and pepper
¾ cup flaked cooked smoked haddock,
(finnan haddie)
½ cup canned whole kernel corn, drained

Fry the bacon until crisp. Drain on paper towels; reserve the fat. Keep the bacon and the fat warm.

Pour some boiling water over the prunes in one small bowl and the apricots in another. Leave to plump up, then drain, pat dry, and chop both finely.

Add the chopped prunes to the bacon fat, stir to coat, and remove. Do the same with the chopped apricots and season both to taste.

Melt the butter in a small pan and add the flour. Cook for a minute or so, then gradually add the milk, stirring constantly, and bring to a boil. Simmer for 2 minutes, then adjust the seasoning. Add the flaked haddock and corn and mix well (it should have a fairly thick consistency).

Slit open the still-warm croissants, place a slice of bacon in each of half of them and fill with either apricots or prunes. Stuff the others with the fish and corn mixture.

Serve while still hot.

Pork Tenderloin

WITH PURPLE SAGE BUTTER

Serves 4
Preparation: 10 mins
Cooking: about 20 mins

3 tbsp good-quality vegetable oil
1½ lb pork tenderloin, cut into
½-inch pieces
juice of 2 lemons
10 sage flower heads, for garnish

for the sage butter:
3 tbsp butter
½ cup chopped tender young sage leaves
1 tbsp lime juice
¼ cup light cream
¼ cup crème fraîche
salt and pepper

Heat the oil in a heavy-bottomed pan over a moderate heat and stir-fry the pork pieces until sealed, then add the lemon juice. Continue to stir-fry for about 8 minutes, until cooked according to taste.

Transfer the well-drained pork pieces to a warmed serving dish. Cover and keep the dish warm while making the purple sage butter.

Melt the butter in a sauté pan over a moderate heat and sauté the sage leaves for 2 minutes. Add the lime juice and stir for about 30 seconds. Increase the heat to high and cook for a further 30 seconds.

Reduce the heat to low and add the cream, and seasoning to taste, then add the crème fraîche. Heat through but do not allow to boil.

To serve, pour the purple sage butter over the pork and garnish with the sage flower heads.

A TASTE OF HERBS
Rosemary, purple sage, chives and dill are attractive not only in their culinary potential – their delicate flowers and foliage make them look almost too good to eat.

Brick-Baked Lamb

WITH LAVENDER AND HAY

Serves 6
Preparation: 10 mins
Cooking: 20 mins per pound for slightly pink lamb, 25 mins for well-done

1 boned leg or loin of lamb, weighing about 4-5 lb
about 24 heads and stems of lavender
bunch of hay (dried grass), about 2½ inches across
1 stick butter, softened
salt and pepper

Preheat the oven to 425°F.

Make 8 shallow incisions all over the surface of the lamb and insert a lavender head into each.

Wash the bunch of hay by holding under cold running water and then shake it lightly to dry it a little, but allow it still to retain some water. Bend the bunch of hay into a nest shape and place it inside a clay cooker (schlemmertopf). Sprinkle the remaining lavender over the hay, reserving a few of the best lavender sprigs for garnish.

Smear the lamb all over with the butter, then season generously. Place the lamb on the hay nest and push it down into the center of it. Spoon 4 tablespoons of water over the lamb and then put the lid in place.

Bake for 20 minutes per pound (for pink lamb, 25 minutes for well-done), removing the lid for the last 10 minutes of cooking. Transfer the cooked lamb to a warmed serving plate.

Carefully remove the hay from the clay cooker, shaking off any juices back into the pot. Strain the juices in the pot into a small saucepan. Bring to a boil and adjust the seasoning if necessary.

Serve the lamb garnished with some fresh sprigs of lavender, with the cooking juices in a warmed sauce boat.

Brick-Baked Lamb with Lavender and Hay (left)

WILD LAVENDER *(above)*

FRUIT AND FLOWERS

Gooseberry Fool

If available, add one large head of elderflower when cooking the gooseberries, to counteract their acidity.

Serves 6
Preparation: 20 mins
Cooking: 10 mins
Chilling: 3 hrs

1 lb (1½ pints) ripe gooseberries
½ cup granulated sugar
¾ cup confectioners' sugar
¾ tsp ground ginger
1 unwaxed orange
2 cups heavy cream, lightly whipped

Trim the gooseberries, then rinse them but do not shake off all the water.

Put both sugars and ⅔ cup of water in a heavy-bottomed saucepan over a moderate heat, then add the berries. Bring to a boil, and simmer gently until the berries have cooked to a pulp and the water has reduced. Remove from the heat and allow to cool.

When cool, stir in the ginger, then purée the pulp in a blender. To remove the seeds, strain through a nylon sieve into a bowl. Grate 1 tsp peel and squeeze 1 tsp juice from the orange. Add the peel and juice to the puréed gooseberries, then fold in the cream. Chill for at least 3 hours.

Serve very cold, preferably with light ginger cookies.

Marzipan Strawberries

Strawberries lend themselves particularly well to being transformed in this way because of their firmness and shape. Other soft fruit such as large loganberries or pitted cherries work well, too.

Makes about 12-20
Preparation: 5 mins
Cooking: 20 mins, 4 days ahead

12-20 strawberries, depending on size (see below)
8 oz semisweet chocolate

for the marzipan:

1 cup + 2 tbsp granulated sugar

pinch of cream of tartar

2⅔ cups ground almonds, sifted

½ tsp lemon juice

1 tsp triple-strength rose water (optional)

1 tsp red food coloring (optional)

1 tsp green food coloring (optional)

½ cup confectioners' sugar, sifted

Make the marzipan 2 days in advance: put the granulated sugar and ½ cup water in a heavy-bottomed saucepan and bring to a boil, stirring well to dissolve all the sugar before the liquid actually comes to boiling point. Add the cream of tartar dissolved in a little water. Put a candy thermometer in the pan and then boil the syrup until it reaches a temperature of 240°F.

Remove from the heat and stir in the ground almonds (they must not be at all lumpy), lemon juice, and rose water, if using. Form the paste into a ball. If wishing to color the paste, divide it into smaller balls and color as desired.

Once the paste is cool, knead until smooth on a surface lightly dusted with the confectioners' sugar.

Wrap in waxed paper, plastic wrap or foil, put in an airtight container, and leave for 36 hours.

Choose firm and sweet-smelling strawberries of a uniform size, with the hull and stem intact. The larger they are the fewer you will need (and have the marzipan to cover!). Wipe them clean with a slightly damp cloth.

Roll out the marzipan quite thinly, then cut it into enough 1½-inch (larger for big strawberries) squares, or rounds if

COOL BLUES *(left)*

Marzipan Strawberries LEFT, *Crystallized Petals and Flowers* RIGHT *(p.47) (above)*

preferred, to cover all the strawberries. Mold each piece of marzipan around the pointed end of a strawberry opposite the stem, so that it comes about two-thirds of the way up the fruit.

Melt the chocolate in the top of a double boiler set over a gentle heat. When it is completely melted and still glossy, dip the strawberries into the chocolate to the level desired on the marzipan. Leave them to dry upside-down on a rack.

Rosé and Rose Petal Sorbet

The heady fragrance of roses has made them a favorite ingredient, particularly in oriental sweets and pastries, throughout history. Use old-fashioned rose petals if possible – their scent is much stronger.

Serves 6
Preparation: 10 mins
Cooking: about 20 mins, 24 hrs ahead

3 tbsp triple-strength rose water
24 young pink and white heavy-scented rose petals (plus extra for garnish if desired)
1 cup sugar
2 cups rosé wine (Rosé d'Anjou, Blush or Lambrusco)
2 egg whites

Put the rose water and ⅔ cup of water in a saucepan and heat together until moderately hot.

If the rose petals are older, remove any white heel at their base with scissors. Blanch the rose petals in the liquid for 5 minutes, then refresh in cold water. Drain the petals carefully and pat dry on paper towels.

Put ¾ cup of the sugar in a pan with 2 cups of water and heat slowly until the sugar dissolves completely. Then quickly bring the mixture to a boil, reduce the heat, and simmer for 3 minutes. Remove from the heat and allow to cool.

Add the wine to this cooled syrup, mix, and put in a suitable freezer container. Cover and freeze until slushy, stirring from time to time.

Beat the egg whites until stiff, then add the remaining sugar and beat until completely blended. Add this mixture to the "blush slush" and sprinkle in the blanched rose petals, distributing them as evenly as possible. Freeze the mixture again until firm.

Crystallize the remaining rose petals as described on page 47 and use them as garnish when serving the sorbet.

Note: for those with a sweet tooth, use the rose water to make up the 2 cups of water for the sorbet.

Hazelnut Roulade

WITH BLACKBERRIES
AND LOGANBERRIES

If loganberries are not available, raspberries can be substituted.

Serves 6-8
Preparation: 30 mins
Cooking: 15 mins, plus filling and rolling

7 eggs, separated
1 cup granulated sugar
2 tsp baking powder
2 cups ground hazelnuts (filberts)
2 tbsp confectioners' sugar, sifted
1½ cups heavy cream
1 pint ripe blackberries
1 pint ripe loganberries
1 tbsp crème de mûre or crème de cassis liqueur
sprigs of blackberry stem, for garnish (optional)

Preheat the oven to 350°F. Oil an 11 x 17-inch shallow baking pan and line it with waxed paper (making sure it extends above the sides of the pan by at least 2 inches). Oil the paper lining.

Place the egg yolks in a bowl and beat at moderate speed for 2 minutes. Gradually add the granulated sugar and beat for at least 5 minutes, until the mixture is thick and creamy and ribbons form a trail on its surface when the beaters are lifted out.

In another bowl, add the baking powder to the hazelnuts and mix thoroughly, then add this to the egg mixture. Beat at low speed until evenly blended.

Beat the egg whites until they are just frothy and becoming firm. Add one-fourth of the egg whites to the nut mixture. Continue beating the remaining egg whites until they are stiff, then fold them gently into the nut mixture with a metal spoon.

Spread the batter in the prepared pan and bake for 15 minutes. Allow it to cool.

Remove the cooled cake from the pan, loosening the edges first. Place on the work surface 2 strips of waxed paper overlapping lengthwise to make a big enough base for the cake. Dust the paper with half the confectioners' sugar. Invert the cake onto the paper and remove the lining paper from its underside.

Whip the cream until stiff, then spread it over the cake. Sprinkle this with the fruit, reserving some of the best berries for garnish.

Using the paper to help, roll up the cake, starting from one short side. Transfer to a serving dish and decorate with the reserved fruit and the blackberry stems, if using. Spoon the liqueur over the fruit, dust with the remaining confectioners' sugar, and eat quickly.

THE PERFECTION OF ROSES
A simple arrangement of roses transforms a quiet corner.

Jewel Tart

WITH MARIGOLD CREAM

Serves 8
Preparation: 30 mins, 3 hrs ahead
Cooking: 45 mins

⅔ cup currant (or apricot) jelly
¾ cup fresh red currants, stems removed
½ cup fresh white currants, stems removed
½ cup fresh black currants, stems removed

for the pâte sucrée:
1½ cups all-purpose flour
2 sticks butter, cut into small pieces
¾ cup confectioners' sugar, sifted
pinch of salt
2 egg yolks

for the marigold cream:
2½ cups heavy cream
⅔ cup sugar
4 eggs
3 drops of vanilla extract
petals from 2 heads of calendula

First of all make the pâte sucrée: place the flour on a cool working surface (preferably marble) and make a well in the middle.

Put the butter in the well. Work the butter with the fingertips until softened, then add the sugar and salt, mixing these in thoroughly. Gradually work in the egg yolks.

At this point start drawing in the flour from the sides, mixing well each time, until all is combined.

Work the dough with the palm of the hand until it is even and smooth. Roll the dough into a ball, cover, and chill for a few hours.

When well chilled, preheat the oven to 425°F. Roll out the dough to line a greased 8½-inch round tart pan. Line with aluminum foil and weight with dried beans. Bake for 15 minutes. (Any surplus pastry will freeze well.)

Meanwhile, make the marigold cream: in a bowl mix the cream, sugar, and eggs and whisk them together. Add the vanilla and the petals.

When the pastry case is cooked, remove it from the oven and reduce the oven temperature to 350°F. Pour the marigold cream into the pastry case and cook for a further 25-30 minutes, or until the cream has set. Remove from the oven.

Melt the jelly in a small pan and allow to cool slightly.

Discard any bruised or damaged fruit, rinse in cold water, shake well, and pat dry on paper towels. Scatter the berries to cover the marigold cream completely, then glaze the top with the jelly to serve.

Note: one good way of removing stems from currants is to pull the tines of a fork through them.

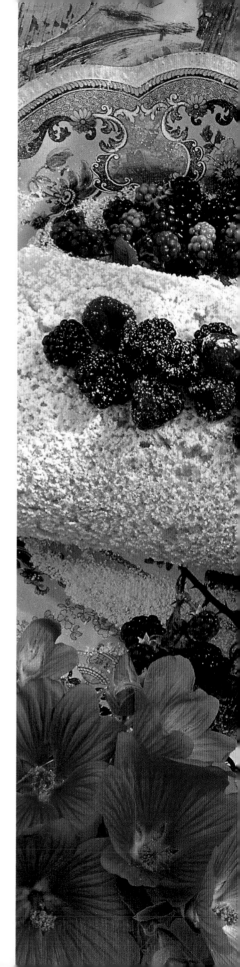

Hazelnut Roulade with Blackberries and Loganberries LEFT *(p.71),*
Jewel Tart with Marigold Cream RIGHT

Autumn

Autumn is throwing on her mantle, a gentle riot of color spanning the spectrum of the artist's palette – pale lime to deep evergreen, copper through to crimson, scarlet and flame, spruce-blue and chocolate-brown, honey-yellow to pear-gold and burnt-orange. Plump, rosy red apples, quince, misty blue sloes, and fat blackberries ache to part company from their life force, tumbling to the ground. Those that escape the eyes and mouths of birds, insects, and animals rest untouched to begin again the cycle of regeneration.

Golden-yellow corn, orange pumpkins, filberts or hazelnuts are all gathered in at harvest time to decorate our churches and tables, to be turned then into nourishing food to soothe bodies that are becoming chillier daily.

AUTUMN MIST (*above*)

FROSTY HEDGEROWS (*previous page*)

Country roads bustle with mechanical life and the business of hedge-trimming, ditch-clearing, plowing, and seeding – sadly, too, spraying. The farming community works against the quickly falling darkness, tending early calves and lambs with a tender eye toward the biting wind and cold, frosty mornings bound to arrive at any time. Squirrels are desperately hoarding walnuts, sweet chestnuts, and acorns. Few escape their beady eyes as they dash from hiding place to hiding place, their ceaseless efforts occupying them from dawn to dark.

Dawn greets us on these cool mornings with the cackling of the crow. Gone is the symphony of summer birdsong – only the resilient little robin sings his heart out through the day. The chaotic chorus of starlings circling in their flock as they search for their bed-time resting place is one of the last sounds as night begins to fall.

With wild plants, grasses, and flowers at the end of their natural life-cycle, collecting seeds is useful. Arm yourself with envelopes and a felt-tip pen and crumble the seeds into an envelope per plant. Label and leave them to dry thoroughly, until planting time in the spring. It brings a real sense of achievement when they appear in your chosen spot. Let children, under supervision, cut wild reed to adorn their own space. Over a six-week period, this beautiful reed changes from black to fluffy white, and, provided it is not moved constantly, will not shed all over the house.

The harvest is the climax of the farming year, and communities throughout the land celebrate this much-loved festival. Pumpkins give delighted children endless hours of pleasure. Traditional, of course, is the Halloween jack o' lantern lit from within with a candle. The seeds which have been removed can be put to good use in the form of jewelry collages or used to make pictures and bookmarks. The flesh of the pumpkin can go into soups and pies for Thanksgiving. Other winter squashes can be baked whole or stuffed.

Wood-burning stoves and ranges and log fires spring back to life after their summer recess, and their smells bring delicious promises of the time to be spent in the warmth of the home and the kitchen. The smell of roasting chestnuts is something not to be missed, especially when snuggled close to an open fire listening to them hiss and pop. Sloes are gathered for the Christmas feasting to come; pears and apples are spiced and canned or made into delicious jams, jellies, and preserves. Blackberries are picked for eating on their

own and in pies, and to make jam; another beautiful hedgerow fruit, the versatile elderflower berry, makes wonderful wine, cordial, and punch.

Big baking potatoes, broccoli and chestnuts, parsnips and pumpkin will be made into nutritious foods so that we can brace ourselves for the possibility of snow, sleet, and cold, freezing fog. Cauliflowers, small squashes, onions, and tomatoes are usually in plentiful supply at this time of year. Pickling is a delicious home-cooking event that can be shared by several enthusiasts around the kitchen table, and presents of homemade pickles are always received with great delight.

Oysters, clams, mussels, and scallops, when bought fresh and eaten quickly, can be simply exquisite. Mackerel pâté, soused herring, and whitebait all make excellent, easy-to-prepare first courses.

Delicious – and deadly – fungi appear in woodlands, fields, and sandy spots. Blewits, shaggy ink caps, parasols, meadow and horse mushrooms, chanterelles, puff balls, and oyster mushrooms can all be found (although once a location is discovered, it is jealously guarded). Positive identification, however, is an absolute must, and hand-washing after picking fundamental.

Game comes into its own during autumn. Roasts, casseroles, and soups take on their own rich flavors, and make a change from the traditional roasted meat. Pâtés also benefit from these special birds and animals. Make braided loaves and fishes, wheat sheaves and mice, inspired by the joyous harvest festival celebrations being held everywhere.

As a novel idea for nibbles, pickle radish, daikon, red cabbage, and celery Japanese-style in 13 parts salt to 1 part water. Leave them for 5 days before eating. These pickled vegetables make an interesting alternative to salted nuts and potato chips.

Purple garlic stripped of outer leaves and drowned in virgin olive oil makes a delicate dressing oil. Make *pilli pilli ho ho* with fresh chili peppers, and use a few splashes to excite a bland soup or stew. Put fresh green and red chilies into a long-necked bottle, then fill it to the top with whiskey. Leave for a week and shake the bottle well before use. When it is empty, fill it up a second time with vodka. You can continue like this, always keeping the same chilies but alternating the spirit each time.

Green walnuts can be picked and pickled; whole almonds toasted, salted, and kept for special aperitif times. Root vegetables can be eaten with gusto after months of crisp summer salads, and tangerines bottled in Cointreau make a superb dessert after a light meal.

Crab apple and Japonica quince make fragrant and subtle jellies, and fresh cranberries are readily available. Make delicious fresh cranberry sauce, maybe adding port or brandy, to enjoy with Thanksgiving and Christmas fare, and now is the time to do battle with the birds for plump blue sloes to make that unmissable treat, sloe gin.

Sloe Gin

Makes two ½-pint bottles

sloes (see below)
2 oz barley sugar or rock candy, crushed
1¼ cups sliced almonds
1 bottle (fifth) gin

When picking the sloes, take 2 bottles and half fill each with the fruit.

Wash the sloes, then prick each of them with a fork and return them to the dry, sterilized bottles.

To each bottle, add half the barley sugar and half the almonds. Fill each bottle right to the top with the gin and cork or screw closed firmly.

Leave to stand, at room temperature, for at least 12 weeks, turning several times to keep the sugar dissolved and redistribute the almonds.

Serve straight from the bottle, allowing one or two of the sloes into each glass. This is a potent drink, so enjoy with care!

Orange pomanders take about six weeks to become hard, so now is the time to start making them. They can then be ready for Christmas presents or decorations, or simply to hang in closets or to lay in drawers.

Orange Pomanders

1 strip of seam binding or plain tape, about 1-foot long
2 unwaxed oranges
toothpick
2 oz whole cloves
½ oz ground orris root
2 strips of pretty ribbon, about 18-inches long and ¼-inch wide

Pin the binding or tape symmetrically around the two axes of each orange to divide them into four quarters.

Make holes with the toothpick and push the pointed ends of the cloves into the skins of the oranges to cover the bare quarters. Leave enough space between them to allow for the skin shrinking as the oranges dry.

Remove the binding or tape, put the oranges in a bowl, and sprinkle them with the ground orris root. Tie the oranges with string and hang them from a coat hanger in a warm room (not an airing cupboard or kitchen as these are too hot). Leave them for six weeks, turning them upside down every 2 days or so (so that the juice flows and the skin does not rot) until they are hard.

Brush off the surplus orris root and tie the colored ribbons over where the tape lay, finishing with a pretty bow on top.

Summery blue skies have changed and the colors are more turquoise. Blustery winds and short, sharp bursts of rainfall leave cloud formations a phenomenon to behold – prehistoric monsters, fleece characters, giant stripes, and whole lands of gloriously designed futuristic buildings sail past on the autumn winds in a constantly changing panorama.

HARVEST TREATS
Pumpkins, preserved fruits and candlelight promise autumn feasts in store.

MENUS *for Autumn*

BREAKFAST
Squash and Ginger Compote (p. 82)
Granary Bread with Grilled Brie (p. 87)
Brioches with Quince and Medlar Preserve (p. 80)
Chanterelle Omelette (p. 88)

LIGHT LUNCH
Broccoli Soufflé (p. 92)
Gooey Meringue with Greengages (p. 99)
Almond Tuiles (p. 82)

LUNCH
Oyster Mushrooms Provençale (p. 88)
Chicken and Paprika Casserole (p. 93)
Pear and Stilton Strudel (p. 97)
Great Aunt Sybil's Apple Crunch (p. 97)

TEA
Carob Fingers (p. 83)
Rosemary and Raisin Buns (p. 82)
Elderberry and Blackberry Jam (p. 80)
Moist Carrot Cake (p. 85)

LIGHT SUPPER
Roast Quail with Watercress and Ginger Wine (p. 93)
Vegetable Julienne with Orange Glaze (p. 90)
Chestnuts in Syrup (p. 87)

DINNER
Pumpkin Soup with Garlic Croûtons (p. 90)
Wild Duck with Nectarines and Grapes (p. 96)
or
Guinea Fowl with Celery and Apple (p. 94)
Glazed Parsnips (p. 92)
Profiteroles with Chocolate and Violet Cream Sauce (p. 100)

PREPARATION

Individual Brioches

Makes 12
Preparation: 30 mins, plus 1½ hrs rising
Cooking: 20 mins, plus cooling

2 envelopes active dry yeast or
¾ oz compressed yeast
2½ tbsp sugar
4½ cups all-purpose flour, sifted
1 tsp salt
4 eggs, beaten + 1 extra yolk
1½ sticks butter, softened
3 tbsp cream

Place the yeast and 1 teaspoon of sugar in a bowl. (Omit the sugar if using fresh yeast.) Add ½ cup lukewarm water, stir gently, and leave in a warm place until the mixture becomes frothy.

Mix the remaining sugar with the flour and salt in a bowl. Make a well in the center and add the 4 eggs and the yeast mixture. Gradually incorporate the flour from the edges and mix to a smooth dough. Remove the dough from the bowl and place on a lightly floured surface. Knead for 5 minutes, or until the dough becomes elastic and feels dry.

Work the softened butter into the dough gradually, a few pieces at a time. Knead again for about 10 minutes, until the dough is very elastic and shiny. Place the dough in a lightly greased bowl and leave to rise for about 1 hour, until it has almost doubled in size.

Remove the dough from the bowl, punch the air out, and knead again until smooth. Divide into 12 pieces.

Grease 12 individual brioche molds with butter.

Remove one-fourth of each piece of dough. Shape the remainder of each piece into a ball and place in the prepared molds. Shape the smaller pieces into balls and put one on top of each larger ball. Brush all over with a mixture of the egg yolk beaten with the cream. Push a wooden skewer through the 2 balls of dough in each mold to keep them in place during cooking.

Glaze again and allow to stand in a warm place for at least 15 minutes, until the dough pieces have doubled in size.

Preheat the oven to 400°F.

Bake for about 10 minutes, then reduce the temperature to 350°F and bake for another 10 minutes until the brioches are golden brown and sound hollow when tapped.

Remove them from the oven, take out of the molds, and allow to cool on a wire rack. (Remove the tops if you are filling the brioches.)

Quince and Medlar Preserve

The delightfully old-fashioned medlar is a rare fruit nowadays and medlar trees are found only in well-established gardens. The medlar's delicate flavor, however, makes it well worth the effort of tracking it down.

Makes about 2 lb
Preparation: 30 mins
Cooking: 20 mins, plus cooling

7 quinces
7 medlars
juice and grated peel of 4 unwaxed oranges
juice and grated peel of 1 unwaxed lemon
1 stick of cinnamon, broken into 2 or 3 pieces
2½ lb (5¾ cups) sugar

Peel and core the quinces and cut them into coarse chunks. Peel the medlars. Cover both fruits with cold water in a large pan. Make sure *all* the seeds are removed before cooking.

Bring the water to a boil, then simmer gently until the fruit is tender. Drain and leave to cool.

When cool, purée in a blender and return to the rinsed-out pan. Add the fruit peel and juice, the cinnamon, and the sugar. Mix well, bring to a boil, and boil rapidly for about 10 minutes until the mixture starts to set.

Remove the cinnamon pieces. Pour the preserve into warm, dry, sterilized glass containers and cover. Label.

Elderberry and Blackberry Jam

This rich and beautifully colored jam keeps well for at least a year.

Preparation: 30 mins
Cooking: 40 mins, plus cooling

equal weights of blackberries and elderberries, washed and stems removed
sugar

Weigh the fruit, then put it in a preserving kettle.

Using both hands, squeeze all the fruit gently. (The color does stain the hands, but it is quite harmless and wears off eventually!)

Slowly bring to a boil, stirring the fruit constantly, then boil for 20 minutes.

Meanwhile, for each pound of fruit, measure 1¾ cups of sugar and warm briefly in the oven (this speeds the gelling process).

Add the sugar to the pan at the end of the 20 minutes and mix thoroughly, then bring back to a boil and boil for another 20 minutes or until gel point is reached.

Pour the jam into warmed, dry, sterilized jars and cover while still hot.

Individual Brioches, Quince and Medlar Preserve

81

Squash and Ginger Compote

Makes about 3 lb
Preparation: 30 mins, 24 hrs ahead
Cooking: 30 mins, plus cooling

2-lb large summer squash or zucchini
4½ cups sugar
¼ cup ground ginger
1 oz fresh gingerroot, peeled
1½ large unwaxed lemons
½ tsp cayenne

Peel the squash with a potato peeler, cut it in half, remove the seeds, and cut the flesh into 2 x 1inch chunks.

Place the squash in a deep bowl and sprinkle with half the sugar, the ground and fresh ginger, wisps of peel taken from the half lemon with a zester, the juice of all the lemons, and the cayenne. Cover and leave for 24 hours.

Put a preserving kettle over a moderate heat and put the squash mixture into it. Cook gently until tender. Add the rest of the sugar and bring very, very slowly just to a simmer, stirring constantly. Cook gently until gel point is reached.

Mash the squash with a potato masher, then put into warm, dry, sterilized jars. Cover and label.

Rosemary and Raisin Buns

WITH CORN AND
BARLEY MALT SYRUP

Makes 12
Preparation: 20 mins, plus 45 mins proving
Cooking: 15-20 mins

1 cup lukewarm spring water
2 envelopes active dry yeast
1½ tsp clear honey
2 tbsp wheatgerm
1⅔ cups all-purpose flour
1½ cups 100% wholewheat flour
pinch of salt
1 tsp dried crushed rosemary
⅔ cup plump golden raisins (unsulfured)
semolina, for dusting

for the glaze:
2 tbsp corn and barley malt syrup or light molassses
or
1 egg yolk
¼ tsp salt

Lightly oil a large mixing bowl and a baking sheet. Sprinkle the latter with semolina. Warm another bowl.

Place the warm water in the warm bowl and sprinkle the yeast on top. Stir in the honey and wait until the mixture becomes spongy. Add the wheatgerm, the flours, salt, rosemary, and sultanas. Stir lightly to form a dough.

Transfer the dough to the oiled bowl and knead it thoroughly for about 3 minutes. Leave in the bowl, cover with a dish towel, and allow to rise in a warm place until the dough has about doubled in size.

Using your fist, punch the dough to release the air in it, then turn it out onto a floured board, and leave to rest for about 5 minutes. Separate the dough into 12 pieces and form them into balls.

Place the balls of dough on the prepared baking sheet, cut a cross on the top of each, and glaze with the corn and barley malt syrup or the egg yolk beaten with the salt. Allow to rise again for about 20-30 minutes. Preheat the oven to 400°F. Bake the rolls for about 15-20

minutes in the middle of the oven.

Serve plain with butter, or with homemade jam.

Almond Tuiles

Makes about 14
Preparation: 8 mins
Cooking: 5 mins

white of 1 egg
4½ tbsp superfine sugar
2 tbsp all-purpose flour, sifted
2 tbsp butter melted
½ tsp vanilla extract
½ cup chopped sliced almonds

Preheat the oven to 350°F and lightly grease a baking sheet.

Beat the egg white to stiff peaks. Then slowly add the sugar a little at a time, beating well after each addition until the mixture is smooth.

Stir in the flour, followed by the melted butter and then the vanilla extract. Mix well.

Place a generous teaspoonful of the mixture on the prepared baking sheet. Flatten with the back of the spoon so that it becomes a round about 2-inches across. Shape 3-5 more cookies on the baking sheet. Sprinkle each lightly with the almonds.

Bake for about 5 minutes, until lightly brown around the edges.

Remove the sheet from the oven, lift each cookie quickly off with a spatula, and lay over a clean rolling pin or narrow bottle. Press the sides gently to mold the cookie into shape. Remove when cool and crisp.

Continue cooking in batches until all the mixture is used. The tuiles store well in airtight containers.

Carob Fingers

Makes about 24
Preparation: 10 mins
Cooking: 10 mins, 3 hrs ahead

4 oz (14 tbsp) each of sesame seeds,
sunflower seeds, and green pumpkin seeds
6 tbsp plump golden raisins
4 puffed rice cakes, crumbled
½ tsp fine sea salt
3 tbsp corn and barley malt syrup or
light molasses
1 7-oz package pure creamed coconut
⅓ cup carob powder

Preheat the oven to 350°F. Spread out the seeds evenly on baking sheets and toast for 10-15 minutes, shaking the sheets occasionally and being careful not to overcook them. Grease a rectangular 7 x 11 in shallow baking pan with oil.

Place all the seeds and the raisins in a heavy saucepan and sprinkle over the crumbled rice cakes and salt. Add the syrup or molasses and mix everything well together.

Gently warm over a moderate heat and stir again. The mixture should stick to the spoon quite firmly. If necessary, add more syrup, but make sure the mixture does not become too runny.

Place in the baking pan, pressing down firmly all over to an even thickness. Bake for 5-6 minutes *only*, until golden.

Melt the creamed coconut in a pan over a low heat, then stir in the carob powder. Allow to cool a little. When the mixture is cool, pour it over the baked seed cake and smooth with a spatula.

Chill for about 30 minutes, then mark out 24 finger shapes on the surface: Chill again for at least 2 hours, or until needed. To serve, slice as required.

GOLDEN SUNFLOWERS AND ORANGES
(*below*)

Moist Carrot Cake (p.85) (*overleaf*)

Moist Carrot Cake

Serves 10
Preparation: 15 mins
Cooking: 1 hr, plus cooling and frosting

1 cup + 2 tbsp sunflower or vegetable oil
1⅔ cups granulated sugar
4 eggs, well beaten
3½ cups grated carrots
1⅔ cups unbleached self-rising flour
1 tsp ground cinnamon
1 tsp ground allspice
½ tsp grated nutmeg
½ tsp fine sea salt
1 cup chopped Brazil nuts
1¼ cups raisins
6 drops of vanilla extract

for the frosting:
1 8-oz package cream cheese
1½ cups confectioners' sugar, sifted
2 heaping tsp grated peel from 1 orange

Preheat the oven to 325°F. Put a circle of waxed paper in the bottoms of two 9-inch layer cake pans. Grease lightly and dust with sugar.

Place the oil and sugar in a blender and combine until smooth. Add the eggs and carrots and combine well again.

Place all the remaining dry ingredients, except the nuts and raisins, in a bowl, mix well, and gradually add the carrot mixture. Finally, add the nuts and raisins along with the vanilla.

Divide the batter between the 2 prepared pans and bake for about 1 hour, until golden. Remove from the oven and leave to cool slightly.

Make the frosting: beat the cream cheese with the sugar and orange peel. Spread half the frosting on top of one cake layer, put the other layer on top, and spread over the remaining frosting.

WOODS AND FIELDS

Chestnuts in Syrup

These nuts in a cognac-flavored syrup are a delightful gift. They also make a lovely light dessert after a rich meal and the syrup is actually good by itself, poured over ice cream, sorbet or fruit.

Fills three 1-lb jars
Preparation: 10 mins, 2 days ahead
Cooking: about 15 mins, several days ahead

1 lb (2 pints) fresh chestnuts
juice of 3 lemons
3½ cups sugar
¾ tsp cream of tartar
½ cup cognac

Snip the tops off the chestnuts and place them in boiling water, a few at a time, for 2-3 minutes. Peel them carefully and remove the brown inner skin. Place the chestnuts in a bowl, cover with cold water, add the lemon juice, and leave to soak overnight.

Drain, then plunge the chestnuts into a pan of boiling water. Simmer until tender but still firm. Drain well.

Put the sugar, cream of tartar, and 2½ cups of water in a saucepan and then allow the sugar to dissolve slowly over a gentle heat.

HARVEST FIELDS
Autumn is a time of intense activity in the farming community, as the year's hard work comes to fruition.

Drop the cooked nuts into the syrup and simmer for 10 minutes. Remove from the heat and leave to stand, covered, for 24 hours.

Next day, remove the nuts from the syrup with a slotted spoon. Put the syrup back on a high heat and bring to a fast boil. Leave to boil until it thickens to a honey-like consistency.

Place 2 tablespoons of cognac in each of 3 warmed, dry, sterilized glass jars. Put the chestnuts in the jars. Fill the jars with syrup and seal while still warm. Immediately turn upside-down to mix in the cognac. Label and enjoy later.

Granary Bread

WITH GRILLED BRIE

This bread can of course be eaten with anything you like, but the combination of its interesting texture and creamy melted Brie is perfect for afternoon tea or a warming brunch. Alternatively, cut each slice into 4 or 8 pieces and serve them as canapés.

Makes two small loaves
Preparation: 10 mins, plus 45 mins proving
Cooking: 20-30 mins, plus cooling

½ cup rye flour
4 cups 100% stoneground wholewheat flour
1 tsp fine sea salt
¾ cup cracked wheat
about 2 cups lukewarm spring water
½ oz compressed yeast or 4 envelopes active dry yeast
1 tsp light brown sugar
1½ tbsp dark molasses
½ lb fairly ripe Brie, cut into ¼-inch thick slices
1 tbsp toasted sunflower seeds (see page 83)

Lightly grease two 5 x 4 x 3 inch loaf pans.

In a large mixing bowl, blend the flours with the sea salt and the cracked wheat, reserving 2 tablespoons of wheat to garnish the loaves.

Warm a small bowl and put ⅔ cup of the warm water in it with the yeast, adding the sugar if using dry yeast. Leave in a warm part of the kitchen for about 10 minutes until frothy. Pour into the flour mixture and then gradually blend in the rest of the warm water. Using the hands, mix thoroughly.

Divide the dough in half and place each piece in a warmed prepared loaf pan. Cover with a clean damp dish towel and leave to rise at room temperature until risen to just above the top of the loaf pan.

Preheat the oven to 400°F.

Bake in the middle of the oven for about 20 minutes. Remove from the oven and paint with the molasses while still hot. Coat with the reserved cracked wheat. Unmold onto a wire rack to cool.

Cut one cooled loaf into slices, toast one side under the broiler, and put a slice of Brie on the untoasted side. Return to the broiler and toast until the cheese bubbles and turns golden. Sprinkle with the sunflower seeds and allow to cool slightly.

Cut each slice into 4 or 8 pieces and serve as desired.

The second loaf will freeze well.

Chanterelle Omelette

WITH CORIANDER

Serves 6 (makes 2 omelettes)
Preparation: 20 mins
Cooking: 5-8 mins

1½ lb fresh chanterelles
2½ tbsp olive oil
10 scallions, trimmed and roughly chopped
(stems included)
juice of 1 fresh lime
½ tsp ground coriander
6 tbsp unsalted butter
10 eggs
sea salt and freshly ground black pepper
1 tbsp chopped fresh coriander leaves
(cilantro)

Remove the stems from the mushrooms, cutting off the small hard piece at the base, and reserve the heads and stems. Wash carefully, dry, and chop finely.

Put the oil in a heavy pan over a moderate heat and add the scallions, lime juice, and ground coriander. Sauté gently for a few minutes. When tender but still crunchy, drain off the liquid and keep the scallions warm in a bowl. Add two-thirds of the butter to the pan and toss in the mushrooms. Sauté until softened. Drain off any liquid (good for stocks) and add the mushrooms to the bowl with the scallions.

Beat 5 eggs with 1½ tablespoons of water until light and frothy. Add half of the remaining butter to a large skillet. When melted and bubbling, add the beaten eggs.

Cook gently over a moderate heat, lifting the sides from time to time to watch for burning. While the middle of the omelette is still runny, add half of the contents of the bowl. Season and add half of the fresh coriander. Gently flip one side of the omelette over the filling.

Turn out the omelette onto a warmed plate, flipping it over to cover the seam. Serve immediately. Make a second omelette the same way.

Oyster Mushrooms Provençale

Serves 4
Preparation: 10 mins
Cooking: about 25 mins

3 tbsp extra virgin olive oil
2 garlic cloves, peeled and chopped
2 onions, peeled and coarsely chopped
¾ lb ripe but firm tomatoes, blanched,
peeled and seeded
2 heaping tsp dried herbes de Provence
¾ lb fresh oyster mushrooms
1 cup dry white wine
1 tsp red wine vinegar
2 tbsp roughly chopped parsley

Place the oil in a heavy-bottomed pan over a moderate heat. Add first the garlic, followed by the onion, then the tomatoes, and finally the herbs, sautéing well for about 3 minutes each.

Increase the heat to high, add the mushrooms, and stir constantly to coat all the ingredients well in oil.

Add the wine and vinegar and allow to bubble for about 2 minutes. Reduce the heat and leave to simmer for about 10 minutes. Remove from the heat. Add the parsley, transfer to a warmed serving dish, and serve immediately.

Oyster Mushrooms Provençale LEFT,
Chanterelle Omelette with Coriander RIGHT

VEGETABLES

Vegetable Julienne

WITH ORANGE GLAZE

This julienne is time-consuming to prepare, unless your food processor can perform this function, but the vegetables look and taste so good that it is worth persevering.

Serves 6
Preparation: 15 mins
Cooking: 5 mins

8 slim carrots
8 slim zucchini
3 small turnips
4 slim parsnips
bunch of scallions
2 tbsp butter
1 tbsp olive oil
½ tsp brown sugar
1 tbsp fresh orange juice
chopped parsley, for garnish

Wash and trim all the vegetables, then cut them into julienne strips, reserving the green scallion tops for the garnish.

Put the butter with the oil in a heavy-bottomed skillet over a moderate heat. Add the sugar, then toss in all the vegetables. Stir-fry for about 2 minutes.

Turn up the heat to high and add the orange juice. Cook for a further 1 minute, stirring to coat all the vegetables evenly with the glaze.

Transfer to a warmed serving dish and garnish with the snipped green scallion tops and the parsley.

Pumpkin Soup

Golden-orange pumpkins are surely the quintessential autumn vegetables – and pumpkin soup one of the most delicious ways of using them.

Serves 4-6
Preparation: 15 mins
Cooking: 15 mins

3 lb pumpkin, peeled, seeded, and cut into chunks
½ lb potatoes, peeled and cut into chunks
6 oz onions
4 tbsp butter
2 cups milk
1 tbsp flour
½ tsp freshly grated nutmeg
salt and pepper
1 cup light cream

Put the pumpkin and potatoes in a large pan of boiling salted water and simmer until just tender. Drain, reserving the liquid, and purée in a blender or by using a potato ricer. Press through a sieve, if necessary.

Sauté the onions lightly in a little of the butter in a pan over a moderate heat. Liquidize in the blender and add them to the purée.

Bring ⅔ cup of the milk to a boil in a pan and melt the remaining butter in another. Add the flour to the butter and cook over a moderate heat for about 5 minutes, stirring constantly. Add the nutmeg and a pinch of pepper.

Pour in the hot milk, a little at a time, stirring constantly. Then add the purée. Bring to a boil, then allow to simmer gently for 5 minutes. Remove from the heat and leave to cool.

Add 2 cups of the reserved vegetable cooling liquid. Return to the blender and purée again. Put back in the saucepan with the remaining milk and the cream and heat gently. Do *not* allow to boil! Serve immediately.

Garlic Croûtons

Serves 6
Preparation: 10 mins
Cooking: 10 mins

4 tbsp butter
¼ cup vegetable oil
3 garlic cloves, peeled and finely chopped
4 large slices of brown or white bread, cut into small cubes (with crusts)

Melt the butter with the oil in a skillet set over a moderate heat. Add the garlic and cook slowly until just golden.

Toss in the cubes of bread, turn up the heat to high, and cook, stirring constantly, until the croûtons are all well covered in garlic and oil and have turned golden.

Drain on paper towels, if wished, and serve in, or to accompany, soup.

Vegetable Julienne with Orange Glaze LEFT,
Pumpkin Soup with Garlic Croûtons RIGHT

Glazed Parsnips

Serves 6
Preparation: 20 mins
Cooking: 30 mins

12 large parsnips
1 tsp kosher salt
1 tbsp zest and 1 tbsp juice from 1 orange
1 tbsp corn or olive oil
1½ tbsp light brown sugar
1 tbsp soy sauce (preferably shoyu)

Preheat the oven to 450°F. Scrub the parsnips, but do not peel. Trim as necessary. Place in a pan of boiling water with the kosher salt. Boil for 10 minutes.

Put the remaining ingredients in a large oval flameproof baking dish. Place over a moderate heat and stir until well combined.

Drain the parsnips and cut them in half, then roll them in the mixture in the baking dish until well coated. Bake for 20 minutes, turning once.

Broccoli Soufflé

Serves 8
Preparation: 10 mins
Cooking: about 40 mins

½ lb broccoli, washed and trimmed
6 tbsp unsalted butter
2 tbsp flour
1¼ cups milk
6 eggs, separated
cayenne
1 tsp freshly grated nutmeg
1 cup freshly grated Parmesan cheese
salt

Preheat the oven to 375F° and generously grease a 2-quart soufflé dish with butter.

Steam the broccoli until tender but still quite crisp. Allow to cool a little then chop into small pieces.

Melt the butter in a heavy-bottomed pan over a low heat. Add the flour and turn up the heat a little. Stir constantly over a moderate heat for at least 1 minute. Slowly add the milk and stir until the mixture thickens. Beat the egg yolks into the sauce one at a time. Stir in the broccoli, a pinch of cayenne, the nutmeg, and the Parmesan. Season to taste with salt.

Beat the egg whites to stiff peaks, then fold gently into the broccoli mixture. Quickly turn the mixture into the prepared dish and bake for 30-40 minutes, until golden brown. Serve immediately.

GOURDS

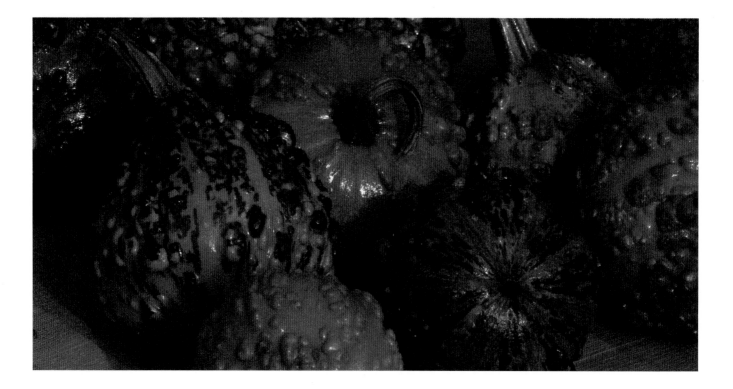

POULTRY AND GAME

Chicken and Paprika Casserole

This is a luxuriously rich, creamy dish, guaranteed to warm chilly autumn bones with its spicy paprika seasoning. Some light vegetables, perhaps stir-fried, steamed or boiled, are all the casserole needs to accompany it.

Serves 4-6
Preparation: 15 mins
Cooking: about 2 hrs

4 tbsp butter
1 tbsp olive oil
1 chicken, preferably free-range, dressed weight about 4 lb, cut into 8 pieces
¼ lb onions, peeled and sliced
¼ lb celery, trimmed and cut into 1-inch chunks
½ tsp dried herbes de Provence
2 tsp paprika
1 tbsp flour
2 cups vegetable stock
salt and pepper
¼ lb carrots, washed and sliced
¼ lb button mushrooms
2 cups light cream

Preheat the oven to 375°F. Melt the butter with the oil in a heavy-bottomed pan over a moderate heat. Lightly brown the pieces of chicken for about 10 minutes, then transfer to a casserole, keeping the fat in the pan.

Place the onions, celery, herbs, and paprika in the fat and toss gently over the heat for about 6 minutes until the onions are just translucent.

Sprinkle with the flour and cook for a further 2 minutes. Gradually add the stock to the pan and bring to a boil. Adjust the seasoning. Pour the mixture into the casserole.

Place the carrots on top of the chicken, cover tightly, and cook in the oven for 1½ hours.

After about 1 hour of cooking, remove from the oven, add the mushrooms and stir. Re-cover and put back in the oven for the remaining cooking time, reducing the heat to 350°F. Five minutes before the end, add the cream and stir.

Serve straight from the casserole accompanied by fresh green vegetables and some boiled potatoes sprinkled with chopped parsley.

Roast Quail

WITH WATERCRESS AND GINGER WINE

Serves 6
Preparation: 10 mins
Cooking: 30 mins

6 quail, dressed
2 large bunches of watercress, coarsely chopped
⅔ cup vegetable stock
1 stick butter
1 cup chopped parsley
⅓ cup chopped onion
2 heaping tsp grated peel from an unwaxed lemon
2 tbsp good-quality nut oil
salt and pepper
1½ cups fried bread crumbs (made from a mixture of brown and white bread)
2 tbsp ginger wine

Preheat the oven to 400°F and rinse the cavities of the birds.

Put the watercress in a pan with the stock, bring to a boil, and leave to cool. Once cool, liquidize in a blender.

Mix the butter, parsley, onion, and lemon peel into a paste and put this inside the cavities of the birds. Paint the outsides of the birds with the nut oil and sprinkle them with salt and pepper.

Place the birds in a roasting pan and roast for 25 minutes, basting constantly. Remove the pan from the oven and tip up the birds to empty their juices into the pan. Place the birds on a warmed serving dish and surround with the fried bread crumbs.

Place the roasting pan over a high heat, add the watercress purée, and bring to a boil, stirring constantly. Add the ginger wine and adjust the seasoning if necessary. Serve the sauce separately with the birds.

Guinea Fowl

WITH CELERY AND APPLE

You could use dry hard cider instead of the Calvados in this dish from the Normandy region of France. The result will not be quite the same, however. Ask your butcher for a chicken or game bird carcass to make the stock. Alternatively, you can use 1¼-2 cups ready-made chicken or vegetable stock.

Serves 6-8
Preparation: 40 mins
Cooking: about 1¼ hrs

1 chicken or game bird carcass
2 bay leaves
2 sprigs of parsley
salt and pepper
3 tbsp butter
2 fresh guinea fowl, each cut into 8 pieces
4 tbsp flour
2 onions, peeled and coarsely chopped
3 stalks of celery, trimmed and coarsely chopped (reserve the leaves for garnish)
3 cooking apples, peeled, cored, and coarsely chopped
⅔ cup dry hard cider
2 tbsp Calvados
6 tbsp heavy cream

Use the carcass to make a stock: put it in a pan with the bay leaves, parsley, and a pinch each of salt and pepper. Add just enough water to cover and bring to a boil. Cover, and simmer gently for about 20 minutes.

Preheat the oven to 325°F. Melt the butter in a large deep flameproof casserole over a moderate heat. Dust the pieces of guinea fowl with flour, then brown them in the butter over a high heat, turning to seal them quickly.

Lower the heat and add the onions and celery. Cook lightly for about 5 minutes, then add the apples. Cook for a further 5 minutes. Remove the casserole from the heat. Sprinkle in just enough of the remaining flour to absorb the fat in the casserole. Cook this flour gently for about 3 minutes.

Gradually add the cider, followed by the Calvados and 1¼ cups of the strained stock. Bring to a boil slowly, then leave to simmer gently, covered, for about 10 minutes. If the sauce does not cover the pieces of guinea fowl, add a little more strained stock. Season to taste, then place in the oven and cook for about 45 minutes.

Remove from the oven and transfer the pieces of guinea fowl to a warmed serving dish. Put the casserole over a high heat and bring the sauce to a boil. Reduce the heat, stir in the cream and adjust the seasoning, then pour over the guinea fowl. Serve garnished with the celery leaves.

Guinea Fowl with Celery and Apple

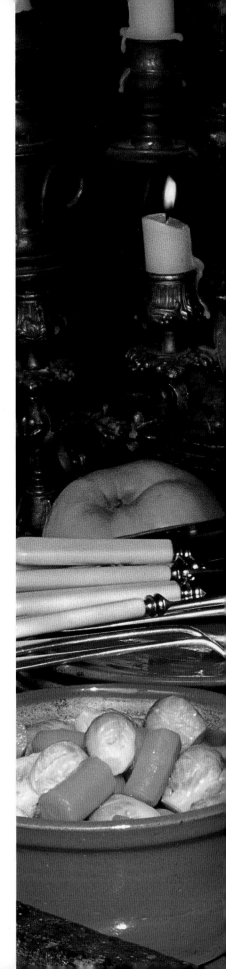

Wild Duck

WITH NECTARINES AND GRAPES

Serves 4
Preparation: 35 mins
Cooking: about 1 hr

2 small mallards, dressed weight about
3-4 lb each, with giblets

t tbsp soy sauce

3 tbsp honey

½ lb red seedless grapes (plus extra
for garnish, if wished)

3 nectarines, sliced (plus 2 extra for
garnish, if wished)

2 heaping tsp grated peel and juice from
1 unwaxed orange

4 tbsp crème de cassis liqueur

⅔ cup shelled pistachio nuts

Prick the ducks all over with a carving fork, to just below the skin, so that the fat can run. Put the ducks, head first, into a large pan of boiling water and boil for 20 minutes. Remove from the pan and drain, breast down, until dry.

Preheat the oven to 475°F.

Place the ducks in a roasting pan and use a pastry brush to coat them liberally with a mixture of the soy sauce and the honey.

Put 5 tablespoons of water in the pan and roast in the middle of the oven for 20 minutes, basting every 10 minutes.

Remove from the oven and baste once more. Reduce the oven temperature to 425°F.

Place the ducks on a wire rack in a clean roasting pan, add 2 tablespoons of water, and roast in the middle of the oven for another 20 minutes.

Meanwhile, put the first roasting pan

FARMYARD FOWL
Geese and chickens make their way through early
morning light.

over a gentle heat on top of the stove. Add the grapes, nectarine slices, and orange peel and juice. Bring to a boil, and add 4 tablespoons of water and the liqueur. Simmer gently until the grapes have just softened (add a little more water, if necessary). Pour the sauce into a warmed sauce boat and add the shelled pistachios.

Give the ducks a final 5 minutes at the hottest oven temperature, then remove from the oven and transfer to a warmed serving dish.

Serve with the sauce, crisply sautéed potatoes, and a dark green vegetable. Garnish with more grapes and sliced nectarines, if wished.

FRUIT AND CREAM

Great Aunt Sybil's Apple Crunch

This is my great aunt's upside-down apple cake. It is at its best and crunchiest when eaten immediately. Alternatively, you can make the cake in advance and fill it just before serving.

Serves 6-8
Preparation: 10 mins
Cooking: about 1 hr

14 tbsp butter, melted
1 heaping tbsp light brown sugar
1½ tbsp light corn syrup
1¼ lb crisp green apples, cored and sliced
juice of ½ lemon
pinch of salt
1½ tsp baking powder
½ cup + 1 tbsp sugar
2½ cups unbleached all-purpose flour
¾ cup evaporated milk
1 egg, beaten
1 cup heavy cream
3 cups cornflakes, crushed

Preheat the oven to 350°F.

Put half the melted butter with the brown sugar and corn syrup in the bottom of an 8-inch round cake pan. Put 1 pound of the apples into the mixture and sprinkle the remaining apples with the lemon juice.

In a mixing bowl, combine the salt, baking powder, ½ cup sugar, and the flour. Add the remaining butter, the milk, and the egg, beating well until thoroughly combined.

Spread this batter over the apples in the cake pan and bake for 1 hour. Remove from the oven, loosen around the edges with a knife, and unmold onto a warm plate. Scrape all the surplus caramel over the apples.

Using another plate, turn the cake right side up, so that the sponge cake part is now on top again. Leave to cool.

When cool, cut the cake horizontally into 2 equal layers.

Whip the cream to stiff peaks. Chop the remaining apples and mix into the cream with the cornflakes. Use this to put the cake layers back together. Sprinkle with the remaining sugar to serve.

Pear and Stilton Strudel

WITH POPPY SEEDS

Delicate leaves of phyllo pastry, layered with pears and rich Stilton cheese, make this a real special-occasion dessert. Any other blue cheese could be substituted for the Stilton.

Serves 6
Preparation: 25 mins
Cooking: 30 mins

1 lb Bosc pears
juice of 1 lemon
grated peel of 1 unwaxed lime
½ lb Stilton cheese
1 tsp fresh thyme leaves
3 tbsp blue poppy seeds
¼ tsp grated nutmeg
salt and pepper
8 sheets of strudel or phyllo pastry
1 stick butter, melted
1⅓ cups dry brown bread crumbs

Preheat the oven to 350°F. Oil a baking sheet.

Peel and core the pears and cut into ½-inch cubes. Sprinkle them with the lemon juice and lime peel.

Crumble the Stilton onto the pears and add the thyme, poppy seeds (reserving a few for garnish), and nutmeg. Season the mixture to taste.

Place a damp cloth on a flat working surface and place 2 sheets of pastry on it. Brush with melted butter and sprinkle over one-third of the bread crumbs, followed by one-third of the cheese mixture. Cover with 2 more pastry sheets, and continue with these layers until all the ingredients are used up, finishing with pastry. All layers of pastry should be coated with melted butter.

Using the cloth to help, roll up the layered pastry like you would a jelly roll. Transfer to the baking sheet, sprinkle with the reserved poppy seeds, and bake for 30 minutes. Serve immediately.

COLOR IN THE ORCHARD (*overleaf*)
Ripening fruits and berries add brilliant splashes of color amid lush green.

Gooey Meringue

WITH GREENGAGES

If greengages are not available, other plums can be substituted.

Serves 6-8
Preparation: 20 mins
Cooking: 1½ hrs, plus cooling

1½ cups superfine sugar
5 egg whites
1 tsp cornstarch
1 tsp white wine vinegar
1½ lb greengages, pitted
⅔ cup spring water
1 tsp maple syrup

Preheat the oven to 310°F. Line a baking sheet with waxed paper or foil, (oil foil lightly, if using).

Beat half the sugar with the egg whites at maximum speed until it resembles wet plaster of Paris.

Mix the cornstarch with the remaining sugar and gradually add to the egg white mixture, beating constantly. Mix in the wine vinegar.

Spread this mixture on the prepared baking sheet with a rubber spatula. Bake for 1 hour. Turn off the oven and leave the meringue in it for a further 30 minutes. Remove from the oven. (The meringue should be hard on the outside, but the inside will have the consistency of marshmallow.)

Place the fruit in a pan and add the water and maple syrup. Bring quickly to a boil and boil until reduced by half. Remove from the heat and leave to cool. When cool, spread on the meringue.

Grape Brûlé

WITH CASSIS

Green, red and purple grapes are combined with a luxurious mixture of cream, crème fraîche and thick yoghurt. The texture of the crunchy caramel – made separately and scattered over the top – is a lovely contrast. You could make a large quantity of caramel and keep the surplus in an airtight container for other desserts.

Serves 6
Preparation: 20 mins
Cooking: about 15 mins, 3 hrs ahead

4 cups sugar
1 lb green seedless grapes
1 lb red seedless grapes
1 lb purple seedless grapes
6 tbsp crème de cassis liqueur
1 cup heavy cream
1 cup crème fraîche
1 cup thick unflavored yogurt

First make a caramel: put the sugar and 1½ cups of water in a heavy-bottomed pan and bring it slowly to a boil, making sure that all the sugar has dissolved completely before the liquid actually boils.

Meanwhile, line a large baking sheet with waxed paper or foil (oil the foil, if using).

Boil the syrup rapidly, for about 10 minutes, watching carefully for a color change toward the end. When it goes from golden to dark brown, remove quickly from the heat and pour the syrup onto the lined baking sheet. (It is possible to make about the size required for your dish when pouring the caramel.) Leave to cool.

When completely set, ease up one corner of the paper or foil. The caramel will start to crack.

Wash, pat dry, and halve all the grapes. Mix them well and place flat side down in a large glass dish. Drizzle the liqueur over them.

Mix the cream, crème fraîche, and yogurt carefully with a fork, then whip until creamy. With a rubber spatula, cover the grapes completely with the mixture. Chill.

When well chilled, place the pieces of cracked caramel over the top to serve.

Notes: do not refrigerate after adding the caramel, or it will sweat. Surplus caramel may be wrapped in waxed paper and stored in an airtight container.

Profiteroles

WITH CHOCOLATE AND VIOLET CREAM SAUCE

When arranged in a pyramid with sauce poured over, profiteroles never fail to create an impact. Hand-made violet chocolate creams for the topping of this truly irresistible dessert are available from good department stores and candy shops. You can also experiment with different-flavored chocolates. Any surplus sauce and topping may be frozen and used to fill and frost cakes, etc. You could also use it to add a very special touch to ice cream or fruit.

Makes 36
Preparation: 20 mins
Cooking: 35 mins, plus cooling

1 stick butter
1 cup all-purpose flour, sifted
pinch of salt
4 eggs, lightly beaten

for the filling:
4 egg yolks
½ cup sugar
6 tbsp all-purpose flour
½ cup cornstarch
1¾ cups milk
2 tsp violet flower extract
1¼ cups heavy cream

for the topping:
10 hand-made violet chocolate creams
3½ oz high quality dark chocolate
10 candied violets

Preheat the oven to 425°F and lightly grease a baking sheet with butter.

First make the profiteroles: place the butter in a saucepan with 1¼ cups water and bring it gently to a boil. Continue to boil until all the butter has melted. Add the flour all at once with the salt, beating fast. Continue to beat very quickly until the mixture starts to leave the sides of the pan.

Transfer the dough to a blender and gradually add the eggs, a little at a time, making sure that each addition is completely incorporated before adding the next. The dough should then take on a glossy sheen.

Put the dough in a decorating bag fitted with a plain tube and pipe 1-inch lengths on the prepared baking sheet about ¼-inch apart. Using a wet finger, smooth the points left by the piping tube.

Bake for about 15 minutes, then reduce the oven temperature to 350°F and bake for a further 10 minutes until the profiteroles are golden brown.

Remove the sheet from the oven and puncture each puff with a small, sharp-pointed knife to allow any steam to escape. Return the sheet to the oven and bake for a further 10 minutes to dry them out. Remove from the oven and allow to cool.

While the profiteroles are cooling, make the filling: in a blender combine the egg yolks, half the sugar, the flour, cornstarch and 4 tablespoons of the milk.

Put the remaining milk in a saucepan and bring slowly to a boil. Add this to the mixture in the blender, with it running at low-to-medium speed.

Pour this mixture into the saucepan and put over a gentle heat. Bring slowly to a boil, stirring, and cook until the mixture begins to thicken. Remove from the heat, pour into a bowl, and leave to cool slightly. Add the violet extract and leave to cool completely at room temperature.

Whip the cream to soft peaks, then add the remaining sugar and whip until incorporated. Fold this into the filling.

Make the topping: remove and reserve any sugar flower decorations from the hand-made chocolates.

Place these chocolates and the dark chocolate in the top of a double boiler over a gentle heat and allow to melt slowly. If the mixture is too thick to pour, drizzle in 2 tablespoons of water a little at a time. Keep warm.

Using a small, sharp-pointed knife, pierce the cooled profiteroles near the bottom to create a cavity. Put the filling into a decorating bag and fill the profiteroles with it. Arrange the filled puffs on a serving plate and pour the topping liberally over them. Garnish with the reserved sugar flowers and the candied violets. Enjoy!

Grape Brûlé with Cassis ABOVE,
Profiteroles with Chocolate and Violet Cream Sauce BELOW

Winter

CHILLY DAYS AND WARM FESTIVITIES

In the countryside, the trees are now stripped naked, except for the evergreens which proudly hold their positions, looking around at the bleak landscape. A few berries blaze in the hedgerow and there are the purple fruits of ivy, the last plant to bear fruit, so late in the season. Rosehips fight the frost and the hawthorn bears its berries boldly, side by side with holly. And there is the magic mistletoe. Norse legend has it that when Freya, the Goddess of Love, cried for her lover, the tears that dropped turned to pearls, and a sprig of these pearls was given to her for safekeeping. She hung it between heaven and earth, promising that it would remain harmless as long as it never fell to the ground – hence the tradition of always hanging mistletoe high up.

SPECTRAL SHAPES (*above*)

DUSKY SHADES (*previous page*)

Birds will have a difficult time finding enough food, so suggest that children make a fat cake for the tits, sparrows, and robins.

Fat Cake

½ cup lard or shortening

1 cup crushed graham crackers, and bread and cake crumbs

½ cup peanuts, and sesame and sunflower seeds

Melt the fat and stir in the dry ingredients. Using an old container (margarine tubs suit the purpose well), make a hole in the center of the container bottom and thread 1 foot of string through the hole, tying a large knot underneath to secure it. Spoon the mixture into the container around the string and place a heavy plate on top to press it all down very firmly. Refrigerate for 24 hours, before removing the cake from the mold and hanging it in your garden for wild birds to enjoy. Put it on a tree close to the kitchen for hours of pleasure from their grateful antics.

December heralds a plentiful time of the year in terms of produce available, as the run-up to Christmas becomes a gallop, and the markets are literally stuffed with provisions of every kind. Crisp apples and tangerines, pork, partridge, venison, and plump turkey, goose, duck, and guinea fowl, and an amazing array of fruit and vegetables create exotic and enticing window displays.

Weather permitting, fresh fish should be gracing the crushed ice, and terrines and stews are alternatives to poaching and baking.

Winter is a time for fine food, pleasure, and fun. When the weather turns foul, farmers overhaul and repair machinery during the day. If the sun shines they toil ceaselessly against the fast-fading light, while in the home preparations of all sorts are being made – cranberry sauce and plum pudding, Christmas tree ornaments and cards, mince pies and brandy snap baskets (see page 125). Many of these things can be made in advance to allow a more relaxing time as the great day looms near.

Start gathering holly, ivy, fir, spruce, and pine cones to make decorations for the Christmas festivities. Spray fruits and physalis leaves silver and gold to make centerpieces for your table. Stencil paper napkins with your own designs, or just tie pretty ribbon around linen napkins. Refresh pot pourri and surround candles with small pine cones scented with aromatic essential oils. Place them in guests' bedrooms for a pleasant surprise, and hang up the orange pomanders which will now be ready (see page 78). Throw handfuls of pine needles on open fires to compete with the delicious aromas of the kitchen.

Feed the furniture after weeks of central heating and open fires. Mix traditional beeswax polish to revitalize mahogany, oak, and pine.

Beeswax Polish

3 oz beeswax

1 oz white wax, or ½ standard sized candle

2½ cups turpentine

1 tbsp dish-washing detergent

2½ cups hot water

Over a moderate heat and using an old saucepan, melt the wax. Remove from the heat and slowly stir in the turpentine. Mix the detergent with the water and gently add the wax mixture. Let it cool, stirring occasionally, then put into screw-top jars and label very clearly.

When using, allow the wax some time to sink into the furniture before polishing off with a clean cloth.

Spend a day making homemade chocolates. Most kitchen shops sell the molds, and it is possible to be really creative using endless combinations of your choice. The most important thing is to use only high quality chocolate. Try fresh cream and black cherry, crystallized stem ginger, marshmallow, marzipan, peppermint and fresh fruit, and golden raisins soaked in liqueur. Wrapped in plain cellophane paper and tied with a pretty ribbon, they are a great standby for small gifts and a lovely present to receive. As a special treat, let children, under supervision, make candy apples in the kitchen (see page 108).

After the excitement of the Christmas feasting, marmalade-making and restocking the pantry takes precedence. Seville oranges and other citrus fruits can be found everywhere. As well as the conventional recipe for the most British of breakfast spreads, Seville marmalade (see page 24), be bold and mix citrus fruits for exciting new flavors. Roast sunflower and sesame seeds, bake pine nuts with garlic in good oil, toast dulse (see page 21) and other sea vegetables. Store them all in screw-top glass jars to use on salads, to sprinkle on vegetables, or simply to enjoy as a snack. Make blueberry vinegar from berries which you have dried in the summer.

Blueberry Vinegar

4 oz dried blueberries
white wine vinegar

Place the blueberries in a glass bowl and cover generously with the white wine vinegar, so that it comes at least 4 inches above the berries.

Cover with cheesecloth and leave on a light windowsill for 2 weeks.

At the end of this time, strain the vinegar through a cheesecloth. Pour it into a dry, sterilized jar with a cork or screw top. Add 3 or 4 blueberries to the jar, seal, and label.

Dress up warmly in woolen scarves and coats, fur-lined boots, and weatherproof hats to take brisk country walks. Search for animal tracks and birds' feet marks in the snow or under icy puddles, and then, to allow those blue noses to regain their natural pink, come home to Winter Warmer tea.

Look out of your window at dusk after a cold but sunny day: as the mist hangs a foot above the warm earth, watch the cows and other creatures moving silently through it like a mobile domino game, and listen to the screech owl sending its eerie warning to small mammals on the ground.

Winter Warmer

Serves 4-6

15 cardamom pods
15 whole cloves
1 stick of cinnamon, about 2-inches long,
broken into pieces
7½ cups spring water
3 tbsp clear honey (preferably acacia, lime
blossom, etc)
1½ cups milk
2 tbsp black tea (not perfumed)

Place the cardamom, cloves, and cinnamon in the water and bring to a boil very slowly. Cover and simmer gently for 20 minutes.

Add the honey and then the milk and simmer again for 10 minutes.

Add the tea and allow to simmer for a further 5 minutes. Remove from the heat and leave to infuse for about 3 more minutes.

Strain into warm cups or glasses.

FROSTED LEAVES
Silvery frosts are one of winter's delights.

MENUS *for Winter*

PREPARATION

Candy Apples

You will need wooden skewers or popsicle sticks to hold the candy apples, and colored plastic wrapping adds to their appeal. After coating with the syrup, you can roll the apples in chopped nuts if you wish.

Makes 8
Preparation: 10 mins
Cooking: 15 mins, plus cooling

2½ pints spring or filtered tap water
4½ cups sugar
⅓ cup light corn syrup
½ tsp red food coloring (optional)
8 hard green apples (preferably Granny Smiths)

Put the water in a pan and place over a low heat. Add the sugar and the corn syrup and stir to dissolve.

Turn the heat to high and bring to a boil. If you have a candy thermometer, let the syrup boil until the temperature reaches 290°F. Otherwise, when small bubbles start popping on the surface and the syrup thickens and turns a light golden color, test for "doneness": drop a teaspoonful of the syrup into a saucer of cold water – the toffee is ready if it crackles and hardens.

Remove from the heat, stir in the food coloring thoroughly, if using, and place the pan in a larger pan of hot water to prevent the syrup from cooling too quickly. There must be no bubbles left and the syrup must be smooth before beginning to dip the apples.

Stick a wooden skewer into each of the apples. Tilting the syrup pan slightly, dip the apples into the syrup and turn them to coat evenly all over.

Remove the apples slowly, making sure there are no air bubbles under or in the syrup. (These air bubbles form if the operation is done too quickly!) Repeat until a coating of the required thickness is achieved.

Place the candy apples on a greased baking sheet, putting them down squarely and firmly to form a steady base.

When the candy is hard, wrap each apple in a square of plastic wrap (colored, if possible, for an attractive appearance) and tie around the skewer, making sure the wrapping is airtight. Chill until required.

These candy apples are best enjoyed within 24 hours, but will keep if necessary for 2 or 3 days.

Ginger Beer

It is little more than a generation ago that many people made their own ginger beer.

There used to be a belief that it would bring bad luck if the "starter" was not divided and one half given away each week. Once word gets around that you have such delicious homemade ginger beer, your friends will no doubt want you to revive this custom and supply them with "starters." If you decide to give them the finished product instead, it's fun to search out old-fashioned ginger beer bottles to pour it into.

Makes two 5-quart jars
Preparation: 10 mins, 1 week ahead

7 tsp + 4½ cups sugar
7 tsp ground ginger
juice of 4 lemons

for the "starter":
4 envelopes active dry yeast
1 tbsp ground ginger
1 tbsp sugar

First make the starter: put all the ingredients with 2½ cups lukewarm water into a screw-top jar and mix well. Put the lid on loosely (do not seal tightly) and stand it in a warm place (but not by a window – 65-85°F is ideal).

Every day for the next week, add 1 teaspoon each of sugar and ginger. At the end of the week, strain the liquid carefully through a cheesecloth into two 5-quart earthenware jars.

To each jar add 5 pints of cold water, half the lemon juice, and half the remaining sugar. Top this with 2½ cups of very hot (but not boiling) water in each jar. Seal tightly with cork and leave undisturbed for 1 week.

Note: the sludge retained after straining may be reused ad infinitum. Divide it between 2 jars and add 1 teaspoon each of ground ginger and sugar and 2½ cups of lukewarm water to each jar. Proceed as described above.

Stained Glass Window Cookies

Makes about 18
Preparation: 5 mins, 45 mins ahead
Cooking: about 15 mins

½ cup confectioners' sugar, sifted
1 tbsp milk
1¼ cups all-purpose flour
1 stick butter (or equal parts butter and margarine)
½ tsp vanilla extract
¼ lb assorted boiled candies (including plain colored, striped, etc)

Combine the sugar, milk, flour, butter (or butter and margarine), and vanilla and knead the mixture until it is a pliable dough. Cover with plastic wrap and chill for 45 minutes.

When well chilled, preheat the oven to 400°F. Roll out the dough on a floured surface. Cut it into decorative shapes, or use pairs of assorted cookie cutters (stars, hearts, trees, gingerbread men, etc) in two sizes to cut out shapes.

Cut a smaller and larger version of each shape and press one on the other so as to leave a border of about ½ inch all round. Pierce the top with a tiny hole, if intending to use as a tree ornament or to hang up somewhere.

Place the shapes on a greased baking sheet. In the middle of each shape, either put a single candy or half each of 2 different candies with contrasting colors – be creative with the colors!

Bake for 7 minutes at the top of the oven, then 7 minutes in the middle of the oven, or until the candies have melted. Leave to cool on the baking sheet.

These cookies make a perfect Christmas tree decoration.

Stained Glass Window Cookies

Cranberry Bread

Makes two small loaves
Preparation: 15 mins
Cooking: about 1¼ hrs

1 cup granulated sugar
1 cup packed light brown sugar
2¾ cups unbleached all-purpose flour
4 tsp baking powder
1 tsp baking soda
2 tsp sea salt
1 cup shelled pecans
1 cup fine wheatgerm
grated peel from 4 unwaxed oranges
(about 6 tbsp)
2 cups fresh or frozen cranberries
2½ tbsp corn oil
1 cup fresh orange juice
½ cup warm spring water
2 eggs, lightly beaten

Preheat the oven to 350°F and grease two 5 x 4 x 3 inch loaf pans.

Combine all the dry ingredients together in the bowl of a blender or food processor, using the slow pulse.

Add the mixed liquid ingredients, again using the slow pulse for about 3 minutes so as to keep the fruit and nuts as lumps rather than completely liquidizing them.

Spoon the mixture into the prepared loaf pans and bake for about 65 minutes, or until the loaves slightly come away from the sides of the pans. Remove from the oven, unmold the loaves and cool on a wire rack.

Cranberry Bread LEFT, *Ginger Beer* RIGHT
(p. 108)

VEGETABLES

Bean, Sweet Pepper, and Potato Soup

WITH GARLIC

Serves 6-8
Preparation: 15 mins
Cooking: about 45 mins

3 tbsp butter
1 tbsp olive oil
3 garlic cloves, peeled and sliced
1 large onion, peeled and sliced
2 leeks, washed, trimmed and cut into ½-inch slices
3 sweet peppers (preferably of different colors), seeded and chopped
2½ pints vegetable stock
1 lb potatoes, peeled and cut into small chunks
1 tsp chili powder
1⅓ cups cooked lima beans
kosher salt

Melt the butter with the oil in a heavy-bottomed pan over a low heat. Add the garlic and cook gently for about 3 minutes, stirring constantly. Then add the onion and the leeks. Cook for a further 5 minutes, then add the sweet peppers and stir-fry for 5 minutes more.

Add the stock, followed by the potatoes, and bring to a boil. Reduce the heat and simmer gently for about 25 minutes. Stir in the chili powder.

Add the beans and bring back to a boil. Season with salt and serve.

Winter Salad

WITH WARM VINAIGRETTE

There's no need to forget salads just because it is winter. In fact, many substantial winter dishes cry out for refreshing crisp vegetables to accompany them. You could try Blueberry Vinegar (see page 106) on the salad instead of the vinaigrette here.

Serves 4-6
Preparation: 10 mins

2 bunches of watercress, washed and trimmed
2 cooked beets, peeled and chopped
2 thin zucchini, grated
1 bunch of scallions, trimmed and chopped
2 tbsp chopped pecans
½ tbsp coarsely chopped parsley
6 tbsp hazelnut oil
2 heaping tsp Dijon mustard
1½ tsp Japanese rice vinegar

Mix the watercress, beets, zucchini, and scallions together in a large salad bowl. Sprinkle over the pecans and parsley.

Mix the oil, mustard, and vinegar in a small pan and heat very gently until warmed through, then pour over the salad. Serve immediately.

Phyllo Triangles

WITH ARTICHOKE HEARTS AND ROQUEFORT

Other blue cheeses can be substituted in this recipe, but Roquefort has a perfect affinity with the artichokes. The little triangles make ideal pre-dinner nibbles, or you could serve them as an appetizer. They also freeze well.

Makes about 24
Preparation: 25 mins
Cooking: 45 mins

4 tbsp butter
8 scallions, including green stems, chopped
1 16-oz can artichoke hearts, drained and chopped small
2 tbsp flour
1 cup milk
¼ lb Roquefort cheese, crumbled
salt and pepper
½ lb phyllo pastry
oil, for deep-frying

Melt half the butter in a pan over a moderate heat. Add the scallions (including the stems) and cook gently for about 3 minutes. Add the artichokes and allow to heat through.

Increase the heat, add the flour, and allow to cook thoroughly. Gradually stir in the milk to make a smooth sauce. Remove from the heat and allow to cool.

When the mixture is completely cold, add the cheese and combine gently. Season to taste. Melt the remaining butter gently in a small pan.

Spread out one sheet of pastry and paint with melted butter (the pastry dries very quickly, so keep the rest in the package until ready to use and cover it with a slightly damp cloth when unwrapped). Cut the pastry sheet into 3-inch strips.

Spoon a generous teaspoonful of filling onto the end of each strip. Taking a corner of the pastry, fold it over to form a triangle. Fold that triangle up over the remaining pastry and continue this way until the end of the strip is reached. Trim if necessary. Continue making the remaining triangles in the same way.

Deep-fry the triangles in hot oil, in batches (freeze some for frying at a later date, if preferred). Drain well on paper towels. Keep in a warm oven until all the triangles are ready.

Winter Salad with Warm Vinaigrette LEFT, *Phyllo Triangles with Artichoke Hearts and Roquefort* RIGHT

Serve immediately as a first course or as canapés.

Note: be careful when adding salt, as Roquefort is a very salty cheese.

Baked Onions

Serves 6
Preparation: 5 mins
Cooking: 1 hr

6 medium onions
6 tsp chopped hazelnuts (filberts)
6 tsp hazelnut oil
6 tsp light brown sugar
6 tsp soy sauce (preferably shoyu)

Preheat the oven to 400°F.

Do not peel the onions, but trim them slightly and level off their bases so that they will sit upright in the baking dish. With a sharp knife, cut a deep cross halfway down each onion from the top. Gently force the cavity open, making sure the flesh does not break.

Drop a teaspoonful each of nuts, oil, sugar, and sauce into the cavity of each onion.

Bake in the oven for 1 hour (adding a tablespoon or two of water to the dish, if necessary).

Broccoli

WITH ROASTED DULSE

The sea vegetable dulse (see page 21) may be unfamiliar to you, but it is well worth trying. It is hugely high in mineral content and deliciously crunchy when roasted.

Serves 6-8 as an accompaniment
or 4 as a main course
Preparation: 10 mins
Cooking: about 15 mins

2 oz dried dulse
2 lb broccoli
4 tbsp butter
salt and freshly ground black pepper

Preheat the oven to 400°F.

Put the dulse in a baking dish in the oven and toast for about 10-15 minutes, until crunchy to the touch.

Put the broccoli in a large pan of boiling water and cook for 5 minutes. Drain when tender but still crunchy and toss with the butter and salt and pepper to taste.

Place the broccoli in a warmed serving dish, crumble the dulse over the top, and serve immediately.

Delectable Potatoes

A stuffing of rich garlic cream cheese explains the "delectable" in the title of these potatoes. You could quite easily use any other cheese of your choice.

Serves 6
Preparation: 15 mins
Cooking: 1½ hrs

6 large baking potatoes
5 oz garlic Boursin cheese (or any favorite soft cheese)
1 tbsp olive oil
1 tbsp kosher salt

Preheat the oven to 375°F.

Scrub the skins of the potatoes clean. Using an apple corer, extract a section from the middle of the potato, going in from both ends if necessary. Reserve the pieces extracted.

Into the cavities, stuff the Boursin cheese, leaving enough room to plug the holes with a short piece of the potato which was removed.

Paint the stuffed and plugged potatoes with the oil, then sprinkle them with kosher salt. Bake for 1½ hours.

Baked Squash

WITH PARSNIP, CARROT,
AND POTATO

This is also very good with grated cheese, especially fresh Parmesan, sprinkled over the top.

Serves 4-6
Preparation: 10 mins
Cooking: 1 hr

6 carrots
6 potatoes
6 parsnips
1 large summer squash or oversize zucchini, weighing about 2-3 lb
1 tsp freshly grated nutmeg
salt and pepper
6 tbsp butter

Preheat the oven to 375°F.

Scrub and slice the carrots, potatoes, and parsnips. Parboil them for 5-6 minutes. Drain well and then put them to one side.

Cut the squash in half lengthwise and remove the seeds. Into the cavity of both halves put the potatoes, carrots, and parsnips. Sprinkle with the nutmeg and salt and pepper to taste. Dot with butter, cover with foil, and bake for 50 minutes.

NUTS

Mexican Bollilos

WITH WALNUTS AND OLIVE SAUCE

This spindle-shaped bread is eaten in homes and sold on streets all over Mexico during the festival of the Day of the Dead. It is also left as an offering at the graveside of departed friends and relatives so that the spirits can take the bread when they come back to visit at this time.

Makes 18
Preparation: 20 mins, 3 hrs ahead
Cooking: 25 mins, plus cooling

1 envelope active dry yeast or
½ oz compressed yeast
2 tbsp soft margarine
4 cups white bread flour
finely ground black pepper
2 tbsp graham flour
1½ tsp fine sea salt

for the sauce:
3 tbsp olive oil
4 onions, peeled and sliced
4 large tomatoes, coarsely chopped
½-1 tsp chili powder
salt and pepper
3 tbsp tapenade (olive, caper, and anchovy spread)
3 tbsp crushed young walnuts

Place the yeast in a small bowl and add ⅔ cup of lukewarm water. Soften and stir the yeast in the water, then leave in a warm place until frothy.

Grease a large mixing bowl with the margarine and add the white and graham flour. Stir 1½ cups more lukewarm water and the salt into the yeast mixture. Mix thoroughly, then gradually add to the flour, blending it in with the hands. When all the liquid has been added, the dough should leave the sides of the bowl and be slightly sticky.

Place the dough on a floured surface and knead until it spreads easily and becomes smooth and elastic. Put the dough back into the greased bowl, cover with a damp cloth, and leave at room temperature for about 2 hours, until almost doubled in size.

Punch the air out of the dough with your fist and knead for about 2 minutes. Leave again, covered, for about 1 more hour. (This is a slow-rising bread, and must be allowed its full rising time!)

Preheat the oven to 400°F and grease a baking sheet. Remove the dough from the bowl and knead again for about 5 minutes, then divide in half. Roll each piece into an 18 x 6 inch oblong. Roll these into cylinders and then cut each across into 9 slices. Form a spindle shape from each piece by pinching one end flat.

Arrange on the baking sheet and brush with water. Sprinkle the pepper on top, then bake for about 20-25 minutes, or until golden. Remove and leave to cool on a wire rack.

Meanwhile, make the sauce: heat the oil in a heavy-bottomed saucepan and gently cook the onions until translucent. Add the tomatoes and stir until soft. Add chili powder to taste and leave to simmer for 10 minutes. Season to taste, then stir in the tapenade and walnuts.

Serve the sauce piping hot as a dip, with the warm bollilos.

Variations: pine nuts or pecans may be substituted for the walnuts in the sauce.

Fried Cashews

Serves 6
Preparation: 5 mins
Cooking: 5 mins

oil, for deep-frying
1 lb (3 cups) shelled cashews
½ tsp fine sea salt
freshly ground black pepper (optional)

Set a small, deep, heavy-bottomed pan over a moderate heat. Pour in the oil to a depth of 1 inch.

Allow to heat until hot, then add half of the nuts and stir until they become golden brown.

Using a slotted spoon, remove them from the pan, carefully draining off any excess oil. Place the cooked nuts in a metal sieve, set over a bowl so that any drips of oil can be returned to the pan.

Repeat with the remaining nuts.

Place all the cooked nuts on paper towels and sprinkle with the salt and some pepper, if wished. Serve warm.

Note: the oil, when completely cool, may be filtered and stored in an airtight jar in the refrigerator for reuse. It enhances the flavor of each subsequent cashew cooking (but do not use more than 4 times!).

Mixed Nut Croustade

WITH VEGETABLE AND HERB FILLING

A croustade is a crunchy crust made from breadcrumbs and, usually, nuts. It is a very useful alternative to a pastry crust and can hold any variety of fillings.

Serves 6
Preparation: 10 mins
Cooking: 30 mins

4 tbsp butter, cut into small pieces
1⅓ cups ground almonds
1⅓ cups fresh brown bread crumbs
1⅓ cups fresh white bread crumbs
½ cup sliced almonds
½ cup pine nuts
⅓ cup shelled hazelnuts (filberts)
½ tsp dried herbes de Provence
2 garlic cloves, peeled and minced
freshly grated Parmesan cheese

for the filling:
4 tbsp butter
2 onions, peeled and sliced
6 tomatoes, skinned, sliced, and seeded
½ lb flat mushrooms, wiped clean and sliced

2 tbsp graham flour
⅔ cup milk
⅔ cup light cream
½ tbsp chopped fresh coriander (cilantro)
½ tsp ground coriander
1 tbsp chopped fresh parsley
salt and pepper

Preheat the oven to 450°F and grease a 7-inch round ovenproof dish.

Rub together the butter, ground almonds, and bread crumbs. Then add the other nuts, the herbs, and the garlic and mix thoroughly.

Press the mixture into the prepared dish to line the bottom evenly and come about ½ inch up the sides. Bake for about 15-20 minutes, or until golden brown.

Meanwhile, make the filling: melt the butter in a pan over a moderate heat and sauté the onions and tomatoes until tender. Add the mushrooms and cook for a further 3 minutes.

Add the flour and stir gently for about 4 minutes, then reduce the heat and gradually stir in the milk and cream mixed together. Cook until the sauce thickens, then add the herbs and coriander and season the sauce to taste.

When the croustade is cooked, increase the oven temperature to 475°F. Spoon the filling into the croustade and bake for a further 5 minutes. Sprinkle over freshly grated Parmesan just before serving.

Mixed Nut Croustade LEFT, *Fried Cashews* RIGHT *(p.115)*

Caramel-Dipped Fruit and Nuts

Preparation: 20 mins
Cooking: 20 mins, plus cooling

clementines or tangerines
baby pineapple, peeled, cored, and
sliced into rings
2¼ cups sugar
⅔ cup spring or filtered tap water
Brazil nuts, hazelnuts (filberts), and
macadamia nuts, shelled and skinned
husked Cape gooseberries (physalis)
strawberries, wiped but not hulled
star fruit (carambola), sliced

seedless grapes
chopped crystallized stem ginger (optional)
chopped hazelnuts (filberts) or almonds
(optional)

Peel and segment the clementines, leaving the membrane intact. Cut the pineapple rings into bite-sized pieces.

Very lightly oil a baking sheet.

Place the sugar and water in a heavy-bottomed pan over a high heat and stir constantly until all the sugar has dissolved. Do not allow to boil until it has! Boil rapidly, without stirring, until the syrup turns a golden brown color. Watch attentively!

Remove the pan from the heat and test by dropping a teaspoonful of syrup into a bowl of cold water. The caramel should set instantly. If it does not, boil for a few minutes more and do the test again.

When ready, remove from the heat and dip the nuts and fruit in the caramel, one piece at a time, holding them on wooden toothpicks or skewers. Drain away excess back into the pan. Sprinkle with (or roll in) chopped crystallized ginger or nuts as preferred. Leave to cool and set on the oiled baking sheet.

Do not refrigerate as this will make the caramel sweat.

RAINDROPS ON CAMELLIAS
Flower heads create a spectacular, if short-lived, display.

MEAT AND GAME

Jambon en Croûte

A European alternative to the traditional baked ham. In Italy, this wonderfully festive dish would be served with candied fruits.

Serves 8-20
Preparation: 2½ hrs, 24 hrs ahead
Cooking: 40 mins

1 uncooked ham on the bone, weighing about 6 lb
2 large carrots, peeled and cut into chunks
2 large onions, peeled and quartered
2 stalks of celery, trimmed and cut into chunks
6 whole cloves
1 bottle (75 cl) dry white wine
vegetable stock
½ cup Dijon mustard
1½ lb puff pastry
1 egg, lightly beaten
3 tbsp butter
4 tbsp flour
salt and pepper

Put the ham in a large pot and add the vegetables, cloves, wine, and enough stock to cover. Bring the liquid to near boiling, then cover. Reduce the heat and simmer for 2 hours. Remove the pot from the heat and leave the ham to cool completely in the stock.

When quite cool, preheat the oven to 425°F. Drain the ham, reserving the stock, and cut off any fat from the surface. Coat the ham with the Dijon mustard.

On a cool surface, carefully roll out the pastry to a thickness of about ¼ inch and completely wrap the ham in the pastry sheet.

Seal any edges with beaten egg and pinch closed, then glaze the surface of the pastry all over with egg. Garnish with pastry leaves or flowers, as desired, and glaze these.

Bake on a slightly dampened baking sheet in the center of the oven for 40 minutes.

Meanwhile, strain enough of the stock from the pot to measure 2½ cups. Melt the butter in a small pan and add the flour. Cook thoroughly, stirring well, then gradually add the measured stock. Bring to a boil, stirring, and simmer for a few minutes, then taste and adjust the seasoning.

Serve the ham in thick slices with the sauce passed separately.

Boiled Smoked Pork Butt

WITH HERB DUMPLINGS

The perfect dish for chilly winter evenings.

Serves 6
Preparation: 10 mins, 24 hrs ahead
Cooking: 1 hr

1 4-lb smoked pork butt
1 large carrot, peeled and chopped
2 stalks of celery, trimmed and chopped
1 large onion, peeled and chopped
2 tbsp cider vinegar
salt and pepper

for the dumplings:
¾ cup self-rising flour
½ tsp salt
¼ cup shredded beef suet
¾ tbsp dried mixed herbs

Put the pork butt in a pot and cover with cold water. Add the vegetables and the cider vinegar, then bring slowly to a boil.

Reduce the heat to a gentle simmer and cook for 1 hour, ensuring that the meat remains submerged at all times.

Meanwhile, make the dumplings: mix all the ingredients together well in a bowl. Using as little cold water as possible, a few drops at a time and mixing in with a knife, create a stiffish dough.

Using the hands and working as quickly as possible, mold the dough into 12 uniform little balls. Cover and store in the refrigerator until required.

Fifteen minutes before the end of the cooking time, pop the dumplings into the water and cover the pot again.

At the end of the cooking time, remove the pork butt, vegetables, and dumplings from the stock and arrange on a warmed serving dish. Strain some of the stock for use as a gravy and season it carefully. Serve with boiled potatoes and crunchy green cabbage.

SLOE GIN (*above*)
*This classic country drink is thought to date
back to the eighteenth century, when gin-
drinking was at its peak. Made in the autumn
from deep blue sloes (p. 78), it is ready for
drinking about three months later, or for using
in recipes such as Pork Medallions with Sloe
Gin (overleaf). It is even better if left to
mature for up to a year.*

SNOWY DAYS (*right*)
*Chilly weather outdoors makes fireside feasts
seem even more attractive.*

Pork Medallions

WITH SLOE GIN

This is a delicious way to use sloe gin bottled in the autumn (see page 78). Wild and Brown Rice with Orange and Herbs is the perfect accompaniment for the pork (see right).

Serves 6
Preparation: 10 mins
Cooking: about 30 mins

4 tbsp unsalted butter
2 tbsp olive oil
2½ lb pork fillet, trimmed and cut into ½-inch thick slices
½ cup sloe gin
3 tbsp light brown sugar
1 cup sloes from the gin (or raisins or pitted prunes), quartered
salt and pepper

Heat the butter and oil in a large skillet or flameproof casserole over a moderate heat. Brown the pork slices in batches, making sure they are sealed on both sides. Remove and keep warm.

Reserve the pan juices and pour in half the sloe gin. Stir over a moderate heat to scrape up any caramelized sediment.

Stirring constantly, add the sugar and remaining sloe gin and stir until syrupy. Return the meat and its juices to the pan. Add the extra sloes (or raisins or prunes). Season to taste.

Cover and simmer for about 5-10 minutes, until the pork is cooked to taste. Make a ring of the mixed rice (see right) on a warmed serving plate and put the pork in the center.

Wild and Brown Rice

WITH ORANGE AND HERBS

Serves 6
Preparation: 5 mins
Cooking: 30 mins

1¼ cups wild rice, well rinsed
1 cup long grain brown rice, well rinsed
thinly pared peel of 2 unwaxed oranges or firm-skinned tangerines
12 fresh sage leaves
sprig of fresh rosemary
½ tbsp butter or olive oil
salt and pepper
2 heads of sage leaves, for garnish

Cook the wild rice in plenty of boiling lightly salted water for 20 minutes. Reduce the heat slightly and add the brown rice (adding extra hot water if necessary) and cook for a further 20 minutes.

Meanwhile, cut the citrus peel into julienne strips, put in a bowl, and cover with boiling water. Leave for 5 minutes. Drain well and pat dry.

Place the sage leaves one on top of the other and cut them into thin strips with scissors. Remove the leaves of rosemary from their stem and mix with the sage.

Drain the rice thoroughly and rinse under hot running water. Place in a warmed serving dish and gently mix in the herbs and orange peel tossed in the butter or oil. Season to taste and garnish with the heads of sage.

Venison Fondue

WITH JUNIPER BERRIES

Fondues are a very good way of letting everyone get to know each other around the table and a very easy option for the cook as the guests do most of the cooking themselves! This version has the added attraction of venison with an unusual juniper berry sauce. Other meat, such as sirloin steak, could be used instead of venison.

Serves 6
Preparation: 10 mins
Cooking: 10 mins for the dip

2 cups good-quality corn oil
⅔ cup olive oil
3 whole sprigs of thyme
8 fresh or dried juniper berries
2 lb venison tenderloin, cut into 1½-inch cubes
salt and pepper

for the dip:
10 fresh or dried juniper berries
6 tbsp butter
½ cup diced red onion
2 garlic cloves, peeled and diced
2 tbsp lemon juice

Mix the oils and flavor them with the thyme and whole juniper berries. Leave for a few hours.

Make the dip: dried juniper berries should first be soaked in hot water until they swell, then cooked in boiling water until tender. Crush the juniper berries. Put the butter, onion, garlic, and juniper berries in a pan. Cook gently until the onion is tender, then add the lemon juice and seasoning to taste. Place in a small warmed dish.

Put the venison on a pretty plate and

season well. Leave for 5 minutes.

Remove the thyme and juniper from the oil and discard. Heat the oil to 340°F and keep at a steady temperature on a table-top burner.

Guests spear the venison chunks with a fondue fork or wooden saté stick and cook it to taste in the oil then dip it into the juniper berry sauce.

Pork Medallions with Sloe Gin, Wild and Brown Rice with Orange and Herbs

Grouse Breasts

WITH FRESH CRANBERRIES

Tart cranberries complement strongly flavored food.

Serves 4-6
Preparation: 5 mins, 24 hrs ahead
Cooking: 30 mins

1¼ cups fresh or frozen cranberries
3 tbsp dry sherry
1 tbsp sugar
6 tbsp butter
12 tender young grouse breast halves
salt and pepper

Place the cranberries in the sherry and leave to soak overnight. Next day, remove from the sherry (reserving it) and cook the cranberries in a little water with the sugar until tender.

Melt the butter gently in a heavy-bottomed pan, add the breasts, and turn up the heat to moderate. Toss the breasts in the butter, covering them completely and browning them on both sides quickly, cooking for no more than about 4 minutes in all.

Transfer the breasts to a warmed serving dish. Turn up the heat under the pan to high and put in the cranberries. Add the reserved sherry, bring quickly to a boil, season, and pour over the breasts to serve.

DESSERTS AND TREATS

Quince, Mulberry, and Apple Roll

Serves 6
Preparation: 30 mins
Cooking: 2 hrs

½ tsp ground allspice
½ tsp ground cinnamon
½ tsp fine sea salt
1½ cups unbleached self-rising flour
½ cup shredded beef suet
½ cup apples, peeled, cored, and cut into small chunks
½ cup Japonica quince, peeled, cored, and cut into small chunks
½ cup mulberries, gently washed and patted dry
grated peel of 1 unwaxed lemon
grated peel of 1 unwaxed orange
¾ cup light brown sugar
½ cup unsulfured currants
¼ cup light corn syrup

Put a very large pot of water on to boil.

Put the spice, cinnamon, salt, and flour in a large mixing bowl. Stir in the suet and mix well. Gradually add just enough cold water to make a firm dough.

Place the dough on a cold, lightly floured surface and roll it into an oblong shape about ¼-inch thick.

Arrange the prepared fresh fruit over the dough, leaving a border of about 1 inch uncovered at the sides. Sprinkle the citrus peel over the top, followed by the sugar and currants. Drizzle the corn syrup over the top.

Roll up the dough into a sausage (like a jelly roll) and wrap it in wet cheesecloth which has been dusted with flour. Tie the roll at either end and gently place a tie around the middle with a long loop at the top to facilitate its removal from the pot. Gently lower the roll into the pot of boiling water and simmer for 2 hours, replenishing the water as necessary.

At the end of this time, remove the roll from the water very carefully, unwrap and place it on a warmed serving dish.

Serve with a traditional English custard sauce. Old-fashioned, rich in calories, yes, but wonderful!

Sugared Grapes

The sugaring can be done 2 or 3 hours in advance, but the grapes should not be left in the refrigerator or in a damp atmosphere. You will need some toothpicks to hold the grapes.

Serves 8
Preparation: 15 mins

4 oz red seedless grapes
4 oz purple seedless grapes
4 oz green seedless grapes
2 cups sugar
6 tbsp spring water

Wash and dry the grapes thoroughly.

Place 1½ cups sugar and the water in a heavy-bottomed pan over a moderate heat and stir until the sugar has completely dissolved.

Turn up the heat and bring to a boil. Boil until the mixture thickens enough to coat the back of a spoon. If you have a candy thermometer, the temperature should be 290°F. Remove from the heat, but place in a bain-marie or on top of a double boiler to keep the syrup warm.

Quickly pierce small clusters of grapes with toothpicks and dip into the syrup, then dust with the remaining sugar over a bowl to catch the surplus.

Marie's Wicked Chocolate Mousse

WITH HONEYCOMB

Serves 4-6
Preparation: 10 mins, 24 hrs ahead

12 oz high quality semisweet chocolate
½ cup still spring water
6 tbsp unsalted butter
4 oz block honeycomb
2 tbsp light rum
1 cup heavy cream, lightly whipped

Melt the chocolate with the water in the top of a double boiler set over a moderate heat. When melted and smooth, remove from the heat and cool slightly.

Add the butter, stirring gently, and crumble in the honeycomb in large chunks. Add the rum and finally the cream. Fold well, then pour into a mold and freeze.

Remove from the freezer 2 hours before serving and stand at room temperature.

Serve with almond tuiles and langues-de-chat (see pages 82 and 29).

Brandy Snap Baskets

WITH ANGELICA CREAM

Serves 8
Preparation: 20 mins
Cooking: 5 mins, plus cooling and filling

3 tbsp light corn syrup
6 tbsp butter
½ cup light brown sugar
10 tbsp all-purpose flour
2½ tsp ground ginger

for the angelica cream:
½ cup chopped candied angelica
(see right)
1 tbsp corn and barley malt syrup or light
molasses
1¼ cups heavy cream, whipped to soft peaks

Preheat the oven to 375°F and lightly grease a baking sheet.

Place the corn syrup, butter, and sugar in a heavy-bottomed saucepan over a fairly high heat, stirring constantly. The mixture must not boil, but all the butter should melt thoroughly.

Remove the pan from the heat and stir in the mixed flour and ginger.

Drop generous teaspoonsful of the batter on the prepared sheet, well spaced as the batter will spread. Bake for about 5 minutes, until golden brown.

Remove the sheet from the oven and allow to cool briefly before lifting the cookies from the baking sheet with a pancake turner. Have ready small molds placed upside-down (small coffee cups will do) and place the cookies over them to shape them into baskets while still pliable. Leave to cool completely.

Make the filling: add the chopped angelica and the syrup or molasses to the cream and mix well. Place in the baskets to serve.

Sweetheart Meringues

WITH FRUIT FILLING

Makes 8
Preparation: 20 mins
Cooking: 1¼ hrs, plus cooling

4 egg whites
½ tsp cream of tartar
1 cup + 2 tbsp superfine sugar
½ cup chopped hazelnuts (filberts)
¼ cup chopped walnuts
1¼ cups heavy cream
⅔ cup crème fraîche (optional)
1 star fruit (carambola)
2 kiwi fruit
16 sweet cherries, pitted
16 fresh strawberries
8 shelled hazelnuts (filberts)
8 fresh mint leaves

Preheat the oven to 275°F.

Draw sixteen 3½-inch heart shapes on baking parchment and place on baking sheets.

Beat the egg whites with the cream of tartar until very stiff. Gradually add the sugar, beating constantly. Fold in the chopped nuts gently with a metal spoon to avoid losing any of the air beaten into the egg whites.

Fill a decorating bag fitted with a ½-inch star-shaped tube. Pipe a line of the meringue mixture along the outside edge of 8 of the paper hearts. Pipe the mixture all over the other hearts to cover them completely.

Bake the meringue shapes for 1 hour, with the solid shapes on the top shelf and the outlines in the middle. Remove from the oven and allow to cool. Once cool, remove from the paper.

Meanwhile, make the filling: gently blend the cream with the crème fraîche, if using, and whip to stiff peaks. Spread the cream over the solid bases, place the outlines on top, and fill the centers with the fruit – some sliced, some halved, some whole.

Garnish with the hazelnuts and mint leaves to serve.

Candied Angelica

Although you can buy candied angelica, making it yourself is much more fun and more rewarding than a trip to the local market. It tastes completely different, too.

Preparation: 10 mins, 2 days ahead

Cut some young angelica stems into uniform lengths and boil in water until tender. Remove from the water and allow to cool slightly. Peel off the outer skins, place the stems back in the water. Allow to simmer until they turn green.

Drain and allow to dry. Place the stems in an earthenware bowl or jar and sprinkle in an equal weight of sugar (making a note of this weight). Leave to stand for 2 days.

At the end of this time, boil the angelica and sugar mixture until it is clear and green again, then drain in a colander.

Scatter another equal weight of superfine sugar over the drained angelica. Place the angelica on plates and let it stand until thoroughly dry.

LEFT TO RIGHT *Sweetheart Meringues with Fruit Filling, Brandy Snap Baskets with Angelica Cream, Candy Apples (p.108), Caramel-Dipped Fruit and Nuts (p.118) (overleaf)*

Index